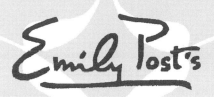

WEDDING PLANNER

THIRD EDITION

PEGGY POST

HarperPerennial

A Division of HarperCollinsPublishers

EMILY POST'S® WEDDING PLANNER *(Third Edition)*.

Copyright © 1999 by Emily Post Institute, Inc.

395.22
POS
5/99

DESIGN BY BTD
PHOTOGRAPHS © ANDREA SPERLING
ILLUSTRATIONS © LAURA HARTMAN MAESTRO

ISBN 0–06–273520–9

99 00 01 02 03 ❖/RRD 10 9 8 7 6 5 4 3 2 1

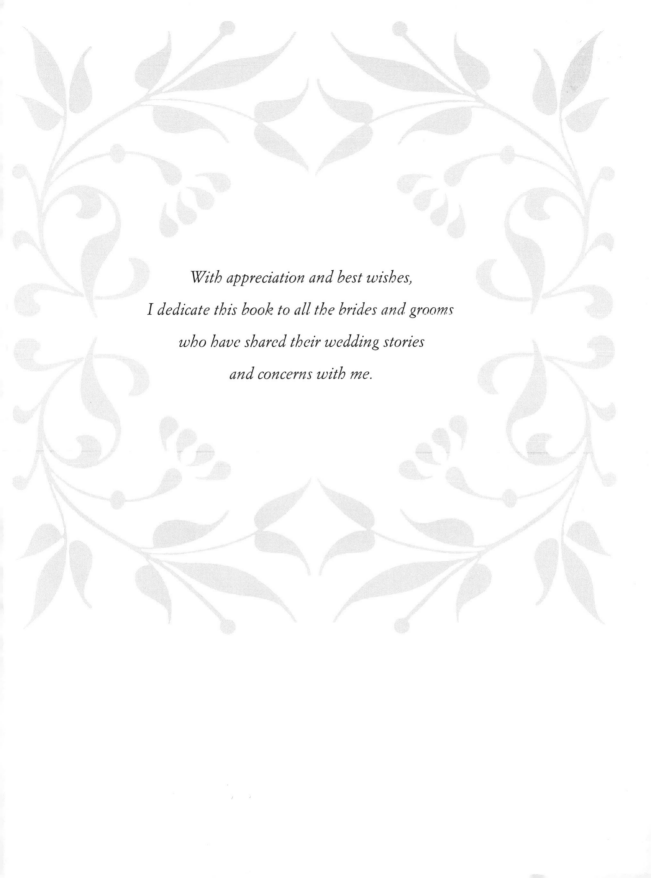

With appreciation and best wishes,
I dedicate this book to all the brides and grooms
who have shared their wedding stories
and concerns with me.

Contents

INTRODUCTION

If you're like most newly engaged couples, nothing quite equals the rapturous thrill of having decided to tie the knot—the excitement of being on the verge of taking one of the most important steps of your lives. But behind the congratulations, rejoicing, and jitters hovers the stark reality of *planning* the big event. How can you get everything taken care of without detracting from the joy and anticipation so unique to a wedding? Having spoken at wedding planning seminars and answered scores of wedding questions in my monthly column in *Good Housekeeping* magazine, I'm well acquainted with the dilemmas that face today's brides and grooms. I'm happy to present *Emily Post's Wedding Planner,* your tool for making the whole process not only manageable but enjoyable.

Before I tell you what the book has in store, you should know that planning your wedding doesn't have to be intimidating. You can bring order to the process by thinking in three broad categories.

1. SETTING YOUR PRIORITIES. Do you want a big, formal wedding or do you lean toward a smaller gathering of family and close friends? Do you want to go the traditional route or put your own personal stamp on the ceremony?

2. TRACKING THE DETAILS. What do you look for when hiring a photographer? When do you time the receiving line—or do you even have one? Do you have any responsibilities for accommodating out-of-town guests?

3. SMOOTHING THE WAY. "Etiquette" means using tact, consideration, and common sense so that you and everyone else, from your attendants and parents to your wedding contractors and guests, feel more comfortable. How do you politely test the quality of a caterer or a band? How can you help your attendants to keep their own expenses down?

Emily Post's Wedding Planner leads you through the entire process, step by step, detail by detail. The planner also serves as an efficient hands-on organizer, with space for jotting down notes on cost estimates, meetings, gift lists, registry information, and even memorable personal anecdotes. Not only will you be able to keep track of your expenses with the planner, but you'll be able to file away receipts, invoices, and memorabilia in handy organizer pockets, which also provide the perfect place to store such items as menu samples from caterers, business cards, proposals from contractors, and mementos from bridal showers and parties. You'll also find time lines, worksheets, and address books—everything you need, conveniently located in one place and under one cover.

The book is designed to answer the questions you already have and raise any that haven't occurred to you. Believe it or not, there's an answer for every wedding question! It's my wish that this trusty planner will help make your wedding as special as you always dreamed it would be. May you relax, get organized, and enjoy!

PEGGY POST
January 1999

THE ORGANIZED
BRIDE AND GROOM

It doesn't take long for chaos to reign if you don't begin with a system of organization. Use *Emily Post's Wedding Planner* to hold all your wedding-related papers, contracts, dress swatches, photographs, and calling cards. You will find everything is easier to manage when you can locate it in a snap. A few tips from the most efficient brides and grooms include:

- Create a MASTER TO-DO LIST, preferably in time sequence.
- Develop a CONTACT LIST with the names and numbers of everyone you're working with. The information can be written down in the "Address Book" that begins on page 245 as you hire vendors and helpers, including telephone and fax numbers and street address (and e-mail address) for each.
- Look for the ADDRESS ICON throughout this planner, as a reminder both to record important addresses in the "Address Book" and to refer to it when you need to find an address quickly.
- Carry a CALENDAR noting all your appointments in the pocket of your planner. Use the Calendar on pages 258–59 to help plan the final weeks leading up to the big day.
- Place copies of ALL CONTRACTS in the pockets of your planner. Don't leave home without these copies in case you have to check details from one supplier when working with another.
- Keep IMPORTANT PAPERS you will need (copies of birth certificate, divorce papers, driver's license) in one pocket.
- Check off COMPLETED TO-DO'S as you accomplish them. You'll feel great as you see the number of check marks grow.
- Use the "PLANNING AT A GLANCE" sections at the beginning of pertinent chapters to help you get organized, and use the "Quick Planner" on pages 255–57 for an overview of what needs to be done and when.

- Carry **ANY PERTINENT ITEMS**—fabric swatches, photos of gowns, photos of locations, table measurements—at all times.

- Look for the **DELEGATE ICON** throughout the planner to help you determine tasks that you can ask a friend or family member to oversee.
- The **SPECIAL REMINDER ICONS** throughout the planner denote tasks that are especially important to take into consideration.

Emily Post's

WEDDING PLANNER

CHAPTER 1

THE ENGAGEMENT

The average engagement period for most couples these days is about 14 months, which offers plenty of time to plan the perfect wedding.

THE ENGAGEMENT:
PLANNING AT A GLANCE

- ❏ The bride and groom announce their engagement to friends and family.
- ❏ The engagement ring is selected if there will be a ring, and if the groom has not already selected it. AS SOON AS THE COUPLE BECOMES ENGAGED
- ❏ An engagement photograph is taken of the bride or of the bride and groom, if the couple is sending one along with the newspaper engagement announcement. FOUR TO TWELVE MONTHS IN ADVANCE
- ❏ An engagement announcement is placed in the local newspaper, if the couple wants to do so. THREE TO TWELVE MONTHS IN ADVANCE
- ❏ An engagement party may or may not be held. OFTEN HELD AT THE SAME TIME THE ENGAGEMENT ANNOUNCE-MENT APPEARS IN THE NEWSPAPER

SPREADING THE NEWS

Even today, most couples rely on traditional ways to share the news of their engagements with their families. It is courteous to tell your parents in person, if you can. Unless you have been married before and have children, you tell your parents first (first the bride's, then the groom's).

If either of you has children from a previous marriage, the children should be told first, even before your parents hear the news. The children's parent should tell them alone, without the future stepparent present. Children of any age need time to adjust to the idea. The future stepparent can be included at another time, to further discuss the engagement and to reinforce that the new relationship will include the children in many ways.

A few key family members and close friends should hear the news first. So that you don't forget or leave someone out, use the following checklist as a reminder.

	BRIDE	GROOM
CHILDREN		
PARENTS		
CLOSE RELATIVES:		
SISTERS		
BROTHERS		
GRANDPARENTS		
UNCLES		
AUNTS		
NIECES/NEPHEWS		
EX-SPOUSES		
OTHER RELATIVES		
CLOSE FRIENDS		

THE ENGAGEMENT ANNOUNCEMENT

In addition to calling and writing family members and friends, you may wish to submit an engagement announcement to your hometown newspapers.

When

Most newspaper engagement announcements appear around two to three months before the wedding day, even if wedding plans have not been firmed up. But there are no hard and fast rules: An announcement may appear up to a year before the wedding date or as little as a week before.

When It's Not Appropriate

An engagement announcement should not be made if either member is still legally married to someone else. Nor is a public announcement appropriate when there has recently been a death in either family or when a member of the immediate family is desperately ill.

Who Makes It

Generally the bride's parents or immediate family announces the engagement, often using a standard form provided by the newspaper. When filling out any form, be sure to include a telephone number so that the information can be verified by the newspaper. The bride's parents should ask the groom's parents whether they would like the announcement to appear in their hometown papers as well. If so, the bride's parents can send it to those papers at the same time that they send it to their own.

Photographs

A photograph of the bride or of both the bride and groom may accompany the engagement announcement. Plan to have your photographs taken at least one month before the announcement appears, to ensure that they will be ready in time and that you are satisfied with the quality of the proofs. You may also want to have extra copies made to give to parents and other relatives.

PHOTOGRAPHER _____ _____

DATE OF DELIVERY _____

NUMBER OF COPIES _____

TOTAL COST _____

Internet Announcements

In addition to sending printed engagement announcements to newspapers, many people are putting the announcements of both their engagement and wedding online. It's easy to do: Several sites, such as the Wedding Help Line (WeddingHelpLine.com), simply ask you to fill out the form supplied and then will post it on their website at no charge for a set amount of time.

Wording

Although each newspaper may have its own simple engagement form to fill out, the information included and the basic content is generally as follows:

> *Mr. and Mrs. Andrew Smith of Evanston, Illinois, announce the engagement of their daughter, Miss Christine Nicole Smith, to Mr. John Paul Rapaglia, son of Mr. and Mrs. Joseph Rapaglia of Greenwich, Connecticut. An October wedding is planned.*
>
> *Miss Smith was graduated from the University of Richmond and is a human resources assistant for Foote, Cone & Belding Advertising in New York City. Mr. Rapaglia was graduated from Mary Washington University. He is at present a member of the New York Yankees baseball team.*

In a small-town newspaper, additional information about the bride and groom's parents may be used.

Wording When the Bride or Groom's Parents Are Divorced

The mother of the bride or groom usually makes the announcement, but as is also the case with a deceased parent, the name of the other parent must be included.

> *Mrs. Donald Pico of Richardson, Texas, announces the engagement of her daughter, Miss Nancy Sasso. . . . Miss Sasso is also the daughter of Mr. Victor Sasso of Providence, Rhode Island.*

When divorced parents remain friends, they may both wish to announce the engagement together.

THE ENGAGEMENT RING

Engagement rings have been around for centuries. In spite of their longevity, it is worth noting that an engagement ring is not essential to becoming engaged. Some couples prefer to use the money that would be spent on a ring toward other purposes; perhaps they plan to buy a ring at a future time when finances permit the expenditure.

Diamonds are the traditional gemstones for engagement rings. But take care before looking to buy, and don't be seduced into spending more than you can afford. Shopping for diamonds should not be an impulse buy; prices and quality can vary widely. Shop smart for diamonds by following the general guidelines below.

- To find a reputable jeweler, ask for recommendations. Shop around before you buy, but when you decide to get serious, ask your friends and family for references. Although you needn't break the bank to buy an engagement ring, the cost can still be significant. Accordingly, you'll want to deal with a reputable jeweler who will do the best and most honest job to find what you want. Find someone who has been in the business a good while, and who is a member of the Jewelers of America or the American Gem Society.
- Beware of jewelers who advertise "wholesale to the public." This is usually a falsehood.
- Make sure the diamond has been graded and certified by an organization such as the Gemological Institute of America. A certification is the written proof of a diamond's weight, grade, and identifying characteristics and should come with your ring.
- Examine the diamond in natural light, rather than under bright fluorescence, to best judge its appearance.
- Once you have selected a ring, make the sale contingent on an independent appraisal. Always ask for a written lab report and a 30-day money-back guarantee, during which time you will have the diamond appraised. If the jeweler declines, take your business elsewhere.
- Study the following primer on diamonds.

SELECTING AN ENGAGEMENT RING

These days, selecting an engagement ring is largely a shared pleasure. Only 30 percent of today's grooms buy a ring on their own, without the bride-to-be's input. This is, after all, the bride's ring, so she may want to be involved in the decision-making process from the start.

An engagement ring is a token of love, but it is also an investment. The more you know, the wiser your investment. These days, the average cost of an engagement ring is $1,300. Following are a few facets of ring buying to help you make the smart choice.

DIAMONDS: THE FOUR C'S

Diamonds are the emblems of love and engagement. Knowing the four C's allows you to converse comfortably with jewelers when you are shopping for a diamond engagement ring.

Carat

A carat is a measure of the weight of a diamond. One carat is one-fifth of a gram (200 milligrams). There are 142 carats to an ounce. One carat also has 100 points. The most commonly affordable sizes are 0.25, 0.50, 0.75, and 1.0 carats—weights that gemologists have dubbed the magic numbers.

Clarity

Diamonds are rated on the basis of blemishes (or inclusions) that occur in nature, such as inner cracks, bubbles, and specks that are hard to detect by the naked eye. The size and placement of the blemishes determine a diamond's clarity rating, which range from flawless, to various degrees of small inclusions, to the least desirable, referred to as imperfect. When a diamond is rated flawless (FL), it is given the highest clarity rating; a flawless diamond is rare.

Cut

The way a diamond is cut indicates its brilliance. In fact, cut is generally considered the most important of the four C's of diamonds. When cut, a diamond is faceted in a series of flat, angled surfaces that reflect light off one another. This is what causes the stone to sparkle.

Color

Diamonds are rated on a color grade scale from D all the way down to Z. If a diamond is clear and colorless, it has a color grade rating of D, the highest color ranking. The lowest rating is Z, indicating a stone that contains slight traces of an earthy color such as brown, yellow, or gray.

GEMSTONES

Instead of a diamond, many couples prefer a gemstone for the engagement ring. Gemstones are classified as "precious" and "semiprecious," with precious stones being emeralds, rubies, and sapphires. Some couples select gemstones for engagement rings based on their birthstones. If you want your ring to symbolize something besides your engagement, you can choose the stone representing your birth month.

JANUARY	*garnet or zircon*
FEBRUARY	*amethyst*
MARCH	*aquamarine or bloodstone*
APRIL	*diamond*
MAY	*emerald*
JUNE	*pearl*
JULY	*ruby*
AUGUST	*sardonyx or carnelian*
SEPTEMBER	*sapphire*
OCTOBER	*opal or moonstone*
NOVEMBER	*topaz*
DECEMBER	*lapis lazuli or turquoise*

SETTINGS

The setting of a ring is the way the stone or stones are arranged within the metal of the ring itself. Two of the most popular settings are:

- TIFFANY. A single diamond perches high on the band.
- ILLUSION. Usually a group of smaller stones surround a larger one.

Two terms often used in describing stones *within* settings are:

- BAGUETTE. Smaller stones, usually rectangular with square corners, set on both sides of a larger, centered stone.
- PAVÉ. Small stones are fitted into tapered holes placed very close together, forming a continuous surface.

RINGS WITH A PAST

Some brides-to-be prefer vintage rings over new ones, as much for their old-fashioned styling as for their romantic history. Vintage diamond rings can be found in antique stores, at auctions and estate sales, and even in some jewelry stores. Heirloom rings often pass from one bride to another in the same family. A bride who is given a family ring as an engagement ring has the choice of simply sizing the ring to her finger or having it reset by a jeweler. If she feels uncomfortable taking the ring, she needn't accept it. An heirloom ring should never be one from the previous marriage of a bride or groom, passed along just because it exists, no matter how many generations it may have been in the family.

STONE SHAPES

Spend some time trying on rings to find the settings and stone shapes that best fit and flatter your hand. The shapes shown here are the most traditional ones.

- **MARQUISE** shapes are oblong with pointed ends. This cut is named after Marquise de Pompadour, the famous mistress of Louis XV.

- **ROUND** shapes are the most popular, probably because their many facets allow them to reflect more light—hence their other name, "brilliant."

- **OVAL** shapes are adapted from the round-cut diamond.

- **EMERALD CUT** diamonds are rectangular with levels, or steps, from base to top.

- **PEAR** diamonds are round on one end and pointed on the other. The round end is worn toward the hand, the pointed end toward the fingertip.

WEARING THE RING

When

A bride-to-be may wear her ring as soon as she receives it, unless she or the groom-to-be is still married to someone else and awaiting a divorce. If an engagement party is planned where a surprise announcement will be made, she may want to wait to wear it so as not to spoil the surprise.

Don't Even Think About It

It's worth repeating: An engagement ring is *not worn* if either of the couple is still married, no matter how close the divorce or annulment may be.

Where

The bride-to-be wears the ring on the fourth finger (next to the little finger) of her left hand. In some countries it is worn on the fourth finger of the right hand. Regardless, it is removed before the marriage ceremony and replaced by the wedding ring, which is worn closest to the heart. The engagement ring is then placed above the wedding ring, closer to the fingertip.

A Good Fit

Whatever the shape or size of the ring you choose, it should be comfortable, allowing your finger and hand to feel unencumbered. It should not be an annoyance nor should you even be aware that you are wearing it; otherwise, the temptation will be to take it off—and then what's the point in having it?

ENGAGEMENT RING: VITAL INFORMATION

JEWELER _____

FINGER SIZE _____ _____

SETTING _____

DIAMOND SHAPE _____

CARATS _____

INSCRIPTION _____

WEDDING RINGS AND BANDS

When to Select

Wedding rings may be selected at the same time as the engagement ring but are more often selected and ordered during the engagement period. Even if the groom has selected the engagement ring as a surprise for his intended, both the bride and the groom should participate in the selection of the wedding rings.

Rings for One or Two?

The bridegroom may or may not choose to wear a wedding ring. If he does, you'll then need to decide whether you want matching rings.

Where Is It Worn?

In the U.S., both the bride's and the groom's wedding rings are traditionally worn on the fourth finger of the left hand.

Types of Wedding Bands

Wedding bands are designed in platinum or yellow or white gold and come in a variety of finishes. If the bride is going to wear her engagement ring with her

---

SPARKLE PLENTY

CARING FOR YOUR RING

Diamonds are easy-care gems and often require little more than a quick polish with a jeweler's cloth. Other gemstones are softer and more susceptible to damage and therefore require more care. Still, there are precautions to take to ensure a long, brilliant life for your diamond.

- Store your diamond when not wearing it in a jewelry case lined with soft fabric, such as felt or velvet, and in a safe place.
- Every so often, soak your ring in a mixture of water and ammonia. Use an old toothbrush to clean around the setting.
- The setting of the stone also requires care, particularly for brides who use their hands in their work. A raised or elaborate setting that can get caught easily or get in the way may not be as good a choice as a more protective setting, such as a bezel setting, where the band hugs the middle section of the stone. Another protective setting is a channel setting, where the stones are set between two strips of the band so that they are held at both top and bottom.
- Be sure to visit your jeweler on a regular basis to make sure the stone is secure in its setting.

KARATS VERSUS CARATS

When choosing which metal is best for your setting and stone, keep in mind that the metal used for the ring itself—usually white or yellow gold or platinum—should always be harmonious with the other elements of the ring. The measurement for the purity of gold in a piece of jewelry is karats. Karats are listed by a number, up to 24. Gold becomes more durable as higher amounts of other metals are blended into it. The purest gold, and therefore the softest and most likely to bend, is 24 karat gold. An 18 karat gold ring is 18 parts gold and 6 parts another metal. A 14 karat gold ring, the most popular, is 14 parts gold and 10 parts another metal. Platinum is a popular choice—it is extremely durable and doesn't wear away as easily as gold. Ask your jeweler's advice before choosing.

wedding band, the two should preferably be of the same metal and work well together.

Engravings

Wedding bands may be plain or engraved with designs on the outside. The inside is usually engraved with words, initials, or simply the date. Ask the jeweler how many letters may be engraved on the inside of your wedding bands so that you can write an inscription that will fit.

WEDDING RING: VITAL INFORMATION

BRIDE:

JEWELER _____

FINGER SIZE _____

BAND _____

INSCRIPTION _____

GROOM:

JEWELER _____

FINGER SIZE _____

BAND _____

INSCRIPTION _____

THE ENGAGEMENT PARTY

An engagement party is entirely optional and may simply be a spur-of-the-moment last-minute gathering of friends and relatives to celebrate your engagement. Other engagement parties are more formal, wherein guests have been sent invitations or a meal has been planned. Although the party may take any form, most often it is a cocktail party or a dinner.

Who Hosts

Anyone may host an engagement party, but it is usually the bride's parents who do so. The host, usually the bride's father, makes the engagement official by proposing a toast to the couple when the guests have assembled.

When

There is no set time to have an engagement party. It may occur before or after an engagement announcement appears in the newspaper. If you wish to surprise guests at the party, however, the party should be held the day before the news appears in the paper. If surprise is not a factor, then the party may take place weeks after any announcement is printed.

The Matter of Gifts

Engagement gifts are never obligatory and not expected from casual friends and acquaintances. They are, however, becoming customary in some parts of the country, given to the couple by family members and close friends. Often, specifically inviting guests to an engagement party carries with it the implication that a gift is expected. If you choose not to receive engagement gifts or don't want to burden family and close friends with additional wedding-related financial obligations, do not announce your news before the engagement party.

The Guest List

The majority of engagement parties are restricted to relatives and good friends, but you may invite anyone you choose. Occasionally the party is a large open house or reception, attended by many friends of both families.

THE BROKEN ENGAGEMENT

If an engagement is broken, the bride should immediately return the ring and all other presents of any value that her fiancé has given her. There is a debate as to whether the ring must be returned if the man is the one who broke the engagement (versus the bride or the couple mutually calling it quits). It makes more sense to return it; why have bad memories of the end of an engagement just to be spiteful? It's better to take the high road—and move on.

Wedding and shower gifts, as well as any engagement gifts, should also be returned to relatives and friends. If it is too difficult to return them in person, they may be returned by mail, accompanied by an explanatory note:

> Dear Rachel,
>
> I am sorry to have to tell you that James and I have broken our engagement. Therefore, I am returning the lovely tray that you were so kind to send me.
>
> Love,
Sara

If the engagement was announced in the paper, a notice may appear announcing that the marriage will not take place. The notice need say no more than "the engagement of Miss Sara Brown and Mr. James Forster has been broken by mutual consent."

On the other hand, should the groom-to-be pass away before the wedding takes place, the bride-to-be may keep her engagement ring, unless it is a family heirloom, in which case she should offer to return it to the family. She can keep any gifts given by relatives and friends but may prefer to return them—especially if they are constant reminders of her loss.

CHAPTER 2

THE BIG DECISIONS

The big decisions are the major choices you need to make as soon as you become engaged regarding the time, style, expense, size, and location of your wedding and reception. From the big decisions come the foundation and framework for all the little decisions to come.

THE BIG DECISIONS

Your initial decisions will be based on the following:

- WHEN? Time of year, day of the week, time of day
- HOW? Style of your wedding (formal vs. informal; traditional, nontraditional, theme); type of ceremony (religious or civil)
- HOW MUCH? The budget
- WHO? Size of guest list and wedding party; officiant; wedding consultant
- WHERE? Locations/sites: ceremony and reception

SETTING YOUR PRIORITIES

To help assess your wedding priorities, please refer to the corresponding chapters in this planner for helpful information. For example, chapter 5, "Guests and Guest Lists," can offer assistance as you decide on your number of guests. In particular, chapters 2, 3, 5, 8, 10, 11, and 12 offer in-depth information to help you with these major decisions. Use the following chart to rank major wedding decisions in order of importance to you. This will help you determine how best to begin planning the big day.

	YOUR RANKING (1–5)	YOUR SPECIFIC WISHES
MONTH/SEASON/DAY OF WEEK		
LEVEL OF FORMALITY		
HOW MUCH TO SPEND		
NUMBER OF GUESTS		
LOCATION		

THE DATE AND TIME OF YOUR WEDDING

TIME OF YEAR

Consider the following when selecting the time of year you choose to wed.

- MOST POPULAR MONTHS. June, September, August, May, October, and July are the favorite months for weddings. Accordingly, the most popular wedding sites (and some honeymoon sites) will be at a premium during those months, in terms of both availability and cost.

- COST-CUTTING ALTERNATIVES. If costs are a factor, you will do better to select a month when rates and fees are lower. In general, the best budget months of the year are January, February, and March. Exceptions: February is high season in the Caribbean, where prices are at their peak. For a destination wedding at a popular tourist spot, such as Disney World or Bermuda, choose the off-season.

- HOLY DAY RESTRICTIONS. Some religions have restrictions on weddings taking place during high holy days such as Lent or Passover. If you are hoping for an early spring wedding, check the calendar—and then check with your priest, minister, or rabbi.

- A WEDDING OUTDOORS. If your vision involves the outdoors in some component of your wedding, you will be limited to warm-weather months, unless you are planning a reception at a ski resort. Even then, a winter ski resort may be fully booked well in advance.

- SCHEDULES: YOURS AND YOUR GUESTS'. Consider the effect your choice will have on family and friends. Think about any hardships your wedding may cause guests who do not live close by.

DAY OF THE WEEK

Consider the following when selecting the day of the week you choose to wed.

- MOST POPULAR DAYS. Most weddings are held on weekends, and for good reason: Weekend days are the customary days off from work. Within the weekends, Christians don't usually wed on a Sunday, their Sabbath, and Jews don't wed on a Saturday, because it is their Sabbath day of prayer and rest.

- COST-CUTTING ALTERNATIVES. A weekday wedding can reap the benefit of lower prices and increased availability of ceremony and reception

THEME WEDDINGS

The increasingly popular theme wedding is just what the name implies: a wedding designed and planned around a specific theme. The theme may be carried over into every aspect of the celebration, from the attire to the food to the decorations. Following are some examples of theme weddings.

- COLOR THEME. The theme of the wedding can be as simple as a favorite color, with the wedding attire, decorations, flowers, and table displays in complementary color combinations.
- VINTAGE ERA THEME. For a Victorian wedding, for example, the bride could wear a Victorian wedding gown and carry a tussy mussy (a nosegay bouquet inserted in a silver, cone-shape holder) or a lacy fan. Lace could be draped from pews and centerpieces, candles lit throughout, and rose petals strewn along the buffet or food stations.
- PERSONAL THEME. Such a theme is often connected to a first or special date or to a couple's favorite shared hobby or pastime. The couple who loves to sail might try a nautical theme, for example, featuring nautical colors and a seafood reception at a yacht club.
- HOLIDAY THEME. For weddings held on a holiday, such as Christmas or Valentine's Day, the holiday traditions could be carried over to all elements of the wedding.
- CULTURAL OR ETHNIC THEME. Those couples with strong ties to an ethnic community might want to incorporate into their celebrations some of the symbols and traditions of their heritage. Some couples who are from different cultures choose to merge the two; for example, the bride might be of Swedish descent and the groom of Greek heritage. Their wedding could include traditions of both cultures.

sites and vendor and supplier access. A weekday wedding, particularly in the late afternoon or evening on a Thursday, is also a logical consideration for a destination wedding, since it provides an entire weekend for guests to fit in a mini vacation along with the festivities.

TIME OF DAY

Consider the following when selecting the time of day you choose to wed.

- **THE MOST POPULAR TIMES**. The most popular booking times are, in order of popularity, Saturday afternoon, Saturday morning, Friday evening, and Sunday afternoon. A late afternoon or early evening wedding is generally the most expensive time to be married. Reception costs are affected as well—if you plan a reception in the middle of the day or anytime from 4 P.M. to 8 P.M., your guests will expect to be served a meal. Plus, the later the wedding, the more formal it is likely to be. The time of day and the wedding's formality, however, aren't necessarily indications of how elegant a wedding will be. Just because you are being married in the morning doesn't mean your semiformal or informal wedding will be any less elegant than one held at night.
- **COST-CUTTING ALTERNATIVES**. A morning or early- to mid-afternoon nuptial is generally less expensive than a late afternoon or early evening wedding. If you are planning to be married during the wedding high season when most sites may already be booked, consider switching your celebrations to a less frequently booked time of day.

THE STYLE OF YOUR WEDDING

There are three categories of weddings—formal, semiformal, and informal. The formality is related to the location of the ceremony and reception, the size of the wedding party, the number of guests, and the time of day. In general, the characteristics of each category are as follows.

THE FORMAL WEDDING: KEY ELEMENTS

- **THE CEREMONY**. The formal wedding ceremony usually takes place in a house of worship or in a large home or garden.
- **ATTENDANTS**. There are usually four to ten bridesmaids and four to ten ushers, in addition to the maid/matron of honor and best man.
- **ATTIRE**. The bride and her attendants wear long gowns in formal fabrics, and the groom and his attendants wear cutaways or tailcoats. Female guests wear street-length dressy clothing for a daytime wedding and usually floor-length gowns or cocktail dresses for an evening wedding. Male guests wear dark suits and ties for a daytime wedding and tuxedos for an evening wedding. An evening formal wedding that requires white tie is the most formal of all.

- **NUMBER OF GUESTS**. A formal wedding usually has 200 or more guests.
- **THE RECEPTION**. The formal reception is usually a sit-down or semi-buffet meal. If the reception includes dancing, music is often provided by an orchestra or full band.
- **INVITATIONS**. Formal wedding invitations are engraved.
- **TRANSPORTATION**. Limousines usually provide the transportation for a formal wedding party.

THE SEMIFORMAL WEDDING: KEY ELEMENTS

- **THE CEREMONY**. The semiformal ceremony can take place in a house of worship, chapel, hotel, club, home, or garden.
- **ATTENDANTS**. The semiformal wedding party usually includes two to six bridesmaids and two to six ushers, in addition to the maid/matron of honor and best man.
- **ATTIRE**. For a semiformal wedding, the bride and her attendants may wear long, ballerina, or tea-length gowns, usually made of simpler fabrics than those for a formal wedding. The groom and his attendants wear gray or black strollers with striped trousers or a formal suit for a daytime semiformal wedding and a dinner jacket with black trousers or a formal suit for an evening wedding. Female guests wear street-length tailored or semi-dressy dresses for a daytime wedding and cocktail dresses for an evening wedding. Male guests wear dark suits for both.
- **NUMBER OF GUESTS**. A semiformal wedding usually has 75 to 200 guests.
- **THE RECEPTION**. The semiformal reception is generally a buffet or a cocktail buffet. The music is often provided by a small band or orchestra or a DJ.

THE INFORMAL WEDDING: KEY ELEMENTS

- **THE CEREMONY**. The informal wedding ceremony can take place in a house of worship, chapel, or rectory or in a home or garden, with a justice of the peace presiding at the latter two.
- **ATTENDANTS**. The informal wedding party usually includes one to three bridesmaids and one to three ushers, in addition to the maid/matron of honor and best man.

The Big Decisions

21

DESTINATION WEDDINGS

Choosing a dream location to marry, celebrate, and even spend a honeymoon is fast becoming a popular wedding choice for engaged couples. Consider the following if you're thinking of having a destination wedding.

- THE PLUSES. A destination wedding is ideal for the couple who wants to hold a small wedding with a few close friends and family in a combined celebration and getaway vacation. It also is a smart solution for the couple who wants both a wonderful honeymoon and a lavish wedding but would have to choose one over the other.
- THE MINUSES. Unless you have the wherewithal to charter a plane for a slew of guests and rent rooms for all of them (customarily, these expenses are the guests' responsibility), you can't expect all of your invited guests to be able to afford to come.
- THE BEST WAY TO PLAN. If a destination wedding is your choice, find a travel agent who specializes in wedding packages. Or work with an on-site resort planner who can make all your arrangements, send you a list of all the documentation you need to take with you, and recommend clergy, reception sites, florists, bakers, and other service providers. A good travel agent or on-site planner can also clear the way for the legalities you need to take care of, from residency requirements to special licenses and fees.

Below are a few types of destination weddings:

- ALL-INCLUSIVE RESORT WEDDINGS. More and more full-service resorts offer complete wedding packages, employing full-time wedding planners to plan the entire celebration, from soup to nuts. All you have to do is show up. If your guest list is large enough, many of these resorts offer reduced group rates.
- TOURISM "HOT SPOT" WEDDINGS. Many of the country's most popular tourist sites and attractions are popular destination wedding locations. Disney World, for example, is fully equipped to handle weddings of all sizes.
- WEDDING AT SEA. Cruise ships are entering the wedding industry with gusto, building chapels and hiring wedding consultants to accommodate the growing number of couples who wish to marry aboard ship. Traditionally, in order to be recognized as legal in the United States, maritime marriages were held in U.S. ports of call. Nowadays, international cruise lines are finding ways to perform at-sea weddings that are legally recognized in the United States, and some captains have the legal authority to perform the ceremony. Before you make any wedding plans, confirm that the cruise line you choose has the legal authority to perform shipboard marriage ceremonies.

- **ATTIRE.** The bride and her attendants wear simple white or pastel floor-length gowns or ballerina, tea-length, or street-length dresses. The groom and his attendants wear suits or sport jackets and slacks. Female guests wear what is appropriate to the location, usually street-length dresses. Male guests wear sport jackets and slacks.
- **NUMBER OF GUESTS.** The informal wedding usually has 75 or fewer guests.
- **THE RECEPTION.** The informal reception can take place in a restaurant or at a home with a caterer and/or friends providing refreshments, usually a breakfast, brunch, or lunch in the morning or early afternoon and an informal buffet or simple hors d'oeuvres and wedding cake for an afternoon reception. Music may come from a single musician or background tapes.

TYPE OF CEREMONY: RELIGIOUS OR CIVIL

Now is the time to decide whether to marry in a house of worship or a secular location. You might want to speak to several different potential ceremony officiants as you make your decision.

THE BUDGET

It's important to discuss finances from the very beginning. Consider the following when working out your budget.

- If your parents are paying for the wedding or contributing to it and have given you a figure that is the most they can spend, it is up to you to work with that amount or combine your resources with theirs. Then tally the projected costs for your wedding and compare it against your resources.
- Keep in mind that for fairly formal weddings, 50 to 60 percent of the costs generally go toward the per-person reception fees. Some caterers suggest making a budget for the reception and then reducing it by 25 percent to cover any overruns.
- Never cut quality to save costs. There are many ways of cutting corners without cutting quality, and we've provided many ideas in the cost-cutting boxes throughout the planner.

The Big Decisions

23

THE GUEST LIST

Keep in mind the following when making up your guest list.

- While your available budget is certainly the determining factor for your wedding, your guest list has everything to do with how the money is spent. Narrowing the guest list is the easiest way to cut costs.
- Ask your families to come up with a maximum guest list, in priority order, with an asterisk by those who absolutely must be there.
- Combine that list with your own lists, and start the process of winnowing the total list, if necessary.

THE AVAILABILITY OF YOUR OFFICIANT

If you place great importance on who performs your ceremony and wouldn't consider getting married without having him or her officiate, check on availability before making *any* decisions about the date of your wedding.

CEREMONY LOCATION

Keep in mind the following when choosing the site of the wedding ceremony.

- If you plan to marry in a house of worship, try to briefly reserve a few dates pending your final decision to be sure the church or synagogue will be available once you have confirmed your reception location.
- If you choose to have your ceremony in a secular location, you will want to consider the range of possible sites, whether indoors or outdoors, in a hotel or wedding hall, at home or at City Hall.
- Your ceremony site choice also depends on whether you want a private ceremony with only a few close friends and family members attending or whether you want everyone at your reception in attendance at the ceremony.

For a further look at selecting ceremony sites, turn to Chapter 10, "Planning the Ceremony."

RECEPTION LOCATION

Keep in mind the following when choosing the site of the reception:

- By the time you have tallied your guest list and determined a date and time for your wedding, you can then focus on the kind of reception you want and your location preferences. Begin checking out sites immediately, in terms of approximate cost and availability. In some parts of the country, reception sites may be booked at least a year in advance.
- Your choice of reception site will affect the type of food you serve, beverages, service, formality level, entertainment, and reception hours.
- Hotels and private clubs are experienced in handling large parties and can do much of the organizing for you. Reception halls with in-house caterers may cost more but can be worth it, considering the ease of service.
- If you're considering a reception at home or at a site where a tent will be used, remember that everything—from the lighting to the flooring to the decorations—will have to be delivered and assembled and then disassembled once the party's over. It can be costly to transform a tent into a ballroom.
- Sites that are bare will require more attention in terms of decor.
- A wedding at a historical site or a botanical garden may be less expensive and require less decorating work but may also require that you use the facility's in-house catering staff or else find a full-service caterer who can work with the facility.

For a further look at selecting reception sites, turn to Chapter 12, "Planning the Reception."

WEDDING CONSULTANTS

More and more couples have full-time careers and a limited amount of time to devote to wedding organization. For busy people with hectic schedules, hiring a wedding consultant is a smart alternative to trying to do it all.

WHAT TO EXPECT FROM A WEDDING CONSULTANT

In general, a bridal consultant can provide the following services:

- Help you decide on ceremony and reception sites.
- Help you select and oversee all the suppliers and vendors you will hire, such as the florist, the caterer, musicians, the photographer, and the videographer.

- Coordinate communication between and among vendors, suppliers, and sites so that, for example, the florist knows when and how to obtain access to the ceremony site.
- Serve as a referee, friend, budget advisor and watcher, etiquette expert, shopper, detail manager, and organizer.
- Coordinate your rehearsal with the officiant.
- Supervise all the last-minute details of your wedding day.

QUESTIONS TO ASK WEDDING CONSULTANTS

When interviewing consultants, prepare a list of questions that will help you evaluate what you can expect of them, and at what cost. These questions include:

ARE YOU A MEMBER OF A PROFESSIONAL CONSULTANT ORGANIZATION?

_____

_____

ARE YOU AFFILIATED WITH ANY SERVICE PROVIDERS? _____

_____

HOW MANY WEDDINGS HAVE YOU COORDINATED? _____

_____

HOW LONG HAVE YOU BEEN IN BUSINESS? WHAT CLIENT REFERENCES DO

YOU PROVIDE? _____

_____

_____

_____

DO YOU WORK ON A PERCENTAGE BASIS OR DO YOU CHARGE A FLAT FEE?

_____

_____

WHAT RANGE OF SERVICES DO YOU PROVIDE? _____

_____

_____

_____

HOW MUCH OF THE WEDDING PLANNING CAN YOU SUPERVISE? _____

_____

DO YOU DELEGATE ANY OF THE RESPONSIBILITIES YOU TAKE ON TO

OTHERS? _____

IF SO, WHICH ONES? _____

_____

_____

_____

WILL YOU BE ON HAND TO HELP ON OUR WEDDING DAY? _____

   AT THE CEREMONY? _____

   AT THE RECEPTION? _____

WILL YOU PROVIDE A ONE-TIME CONSULTING SESSION TO HELP ME GET

ORGANIZED IF I DECIDE THAT'S ALL THE HELP I NEED? _____

_____

CAN YOU PROVIDE A LIST OF YOUR SERVICES AT THEIR INDIVIDUAL

PRICES? _____

_____

_____

WEDDING CONSULTANT NAME _____

_____

ONE-STOP WEDDING LOCATIONS

Locations do exist that offer everything under one roof—ceremony and reception area, food, decor, flowers, you name it—and a wedding coordinator to orchestrate the whole thing. This can certainly translate into ease of service. The pluses of these "one-stop" sites are obvious: For busy couples with a short engagement time, it couldn't be easier. Minuses are the lack of choices and ways to personalize the wedding.

OUR BIG DECISIONS

WHEN

TIME OF YEAR _____

MONTH _____

DAY OF THE WEEK _____

TIME OF DAY _____

HOW

STYLE (FORMAL VS. INFORMAL; TRADITIONAL, NONTRADITIONAL, THEME)

_____

TYPE OF CEREMONY (RELIGIOUS OR CIVIL) _____

HOW MUCH

ESTIMATED BUDGET _____

WHO

SIZE OF GUEST LIST _____

SIZE OF WEDDING PARTY _____

OFFICIANT _____

WEDDING CONSULTANT _____

WHERE

LOCATION/SITE: CEREMONY _____

LOCATION/SITE: RECEPTION _____

THE SECOND LEVEL OF DECISIONS

Once you have settled the who, where, and when of your wedding, it is time to start shopping, interviewing, and booking vendors, suppliers, and services. Because each of these next steps generally requires considerable advance time, there is no time like the present to start.

- Shop for and make decisions about clothing and accessories—for the bride, groom, and attendants.
- Visit stores and list gifts you wish to receive with bridal registries.
- Begin reviewing reception menus.
- Interview and listen to bands or DJs, or start listing songs you would put on tapes for the reception.
- Interview and talk to florists.
- Interview and look at the portfolios of photographers and videographers.
- Order invitations, enclosures, announcements, and other printed material.

THE THIRD LEVEL OF DECISIONS

With all your outside resources in order, you now can turn your attention to the details that will make your wedding day personal and unique. You might do the following:

- Listen to and choose music for your ceremony.
- Select readings for your ceremony.
- Make lists of music choices for your reception.
- Plan special events you want to include, such as your first dance at the reception, a bouquet toss, or a party for your attendants.
- Select gifts for your attendants, perhaps parents, and each other.
- Begin to chart seating arrangements for your reception.
- Incorporate family and cultural traditions into your wedding.

The Big Decisions

CHAPTER 3

EXPENSES

A wedding is an important milestone and as such should be a time of special indulgences. But that doesn't mean paying more than your budget allows for a big, over-the-top extravaganza. You *can* have an elegant, memorable occasion without stinting. In fact, some of the simplest weddings can also be the most beautiful and meaningful. The following is based on the traditional division of expenses and gives you a structure for planning.

WHO PAYS

Traditionally, the bride's family assumes the burden of most wedding costs. Today, however, it is not uncommon for both the bride's and the groom's families to share the costs of the celebration or for the bride and the groom to pay for some or all of the expenses themselves. Modern couples are older and generally employed and independent by the time they get married; some are being married for the second or third time. Many couples not only plan their own weddings but pay for them as well.

TRADITIONAL DIVISION OF COSTS

Below is a checklist of the traditional expense responsibilities of a wedding—*all variable depending on your particular circumstances.*

TRADITIONAL EXPENSES OF
THE BRIDE AND HER FAMILY

- Services of bridal consultant
- Invitations, enclosures, announcements, and postage
- Bride's wedding gown and accessories
- Floral decorations for ceremony and reception, bridesmaids' flowers, and bride's bouquet
- Formal wedding photographs and candid pictures

- Videotape recording of wedding
- Music for church and reception
- Transportation of bridal party to and from ceremony
- All reception expenses
- Bride's gifts to her attendants
- Bride's gift to groom
- Groom's wedding ring
- Rental of awning for ceremony entrance and carpet for aisle
- Fee for services performed by sexton
- Cost of soloists
- A traffic officer, if necessary
- Transportation of bridal party to reception
- Transportation and lodging expenses for officiant, if from another town and if invited to officiate by bride's family
- Accommodations for bride's attendants
- Bridesmaids' luncheon

AVERAGE WEDDING COSTS

The average wedding in the United States today costs close to $19,000. Of that, 50 percent of the costs often go into the reception.

TRADITIONAL EXPENSES OF THE GROOM AND HIS FAMILY

- Bride's engagement and wedding rings
- Groom's gift to bride
- Groom's gifts to his attendants
- Groom's attire
- Ties and gloves for his attendants, if not part of their clothing rental package
- Bride's bouquet (only in those regions where it is local custom for groom to pay for it)
- Bride's going-away corsage
- Boutonnieres for groom's attendants
- Corsages for immediate members of both families (unless bride has included them in her florist order)
- Officiant's fee or donation

- Transportation and lodging expenses for officiant, if from another town and if invited to officiate by the groom's family
- Marriage license
- Transportation for groom and best man to ceremony
- Expenses of honeymoon
- All costs of rehearsal dinner
- Accommodations for groom's attendants
- Bachelor dinner, if groom wishes to give one
- Transportation and lodging expenses for groom's family

BRIDESMAIDS' AND HONOR ATTENDANT'S EXPENSES

- Purchase of apparel and all accessories
- Transportation to and from city or town where wedding takes place
- Contribution to gift from all bridesmaids to bride
- Individual gift to the couple (if being in wedding is not the gift)
- Optionally, shower or luncheon for bride

BEWARE HIDDEN COSTS

Even deciphering the fine print on a contract can leave you with unanswered questions. Know exactly what you need up front so that you can ferret out hidden, unanticipated costs. The contract for a reception site, for example, is based on the length of time your reception lasts, along with all other related costs. Find out what overtime really means before signing the contract. For example, if your reception is planned from two to five in the afternoon, does that mean the bar closes at five and the band goes home and that guests should be gone within half an hour, or does it mean that you have to end the reception by four-thirty to ensure that everyone is out by five? In the latter case, you may be incurring overtime costs if you think the reception literally lasts until five o'clock.

Don't forget taxes and gratuities, which can add a significant amount to the total bill—especially in states that have a high sales tax. It's a good idea to make sure that taxes and tips are included in the total price. And inquire about such hidden costs as "plate charges." Costs such as these can be well hidden in the prices you are charged. You are entitled to know exactly what is included—and what is not—before agreeing to the service. If the service provider or contractor is unwilling to give you a detailed listing or breakdown of costs, consider looking elsewhere.

- Rental of wedding attire
- Transportation to and from city where wedding takes place
- Contribution to gift from all groom's attendants to groom
- Individual gift to the couple (if being in wedding is not the gift)
- Bachelor dinner, if given by groom's attendants

BIG-TICKET COST-CUTTERS

You can economize on big-ticket items by keeping the following tips in mind.

- The best way to economize is to cut your guest list.
- Many wonderful reception sites can be found at much more affordable prices than the costs of traditional wedding facilities. Consider public gardens, historic homes and sites, and museums and aquariums.
- Choose a time of year, a day of the week, and a time of day when prices are not at a premium. If getting married in November instead of October allows you to have the kind of reception you want for a third of the cost, consider it. Generally, prices are at their highest on Saturdays and in the late afternoon and evening. Reduce expenses by having a Saturday morning wedding instead of a Saturday evening one. This frees up money you've allocated for reception costs, often a whopping 50 percent of a wedding budget.
- Avoid paying for extras you don't want. For example, a band that charges for a master of ceremonies when you don't want a master of ceremonies is not a good value, just as a reception package that includes printed napkins and matchbooks has less value if you don't care about these incidentals.
- Let friends help, with the understanding that their service is their wedding gift to you. If your attendants can stay with friends and family, this saves your having to pay expensive hotel or motel costs.
- Check Internet websites for discount or wholesale bridal services. You can locate services that offer discount designer bridal and attendant gowns, discount china and silver patterns, and discount printed items.
- Comparison shop. Don't just hire the first vendor you find in the telephone book. Ask about services before you sign any contract. By the time you have interviewed three or more companies, you will have a pretty good idea of what you need to know to make your decision.
- Consider a wedding consultant. One of the values of using wedding consultants is that they often have access to quality services at the best prices from vendors and suppliers. They may also receive frequent-user discounts from suppliers.

OUT-OF-TOWN GUESTS' EXPENSES

- Transportation to and from wedding
- Lodging expenses
- Wedding gift

DETERMINING A BUDGET

Your budget should include allotments for each of the expenses listed below. Begin with a dollar amount of what you believe you can spend on your wedding. Calculate your absolute fixed costs, such as the minister's or rabbi's fee, the postage required for the wedding invitations, and the marriage license. Then add in the expected costs of your essential wedding expenses, such as the wedding dress, wedding rings, and gifts for the attendants. Finally, once you have determined your mandatory costs, subtract that total from your available funds and see what amount you have left to work with. This will give you a guide as to how much you have for variable costs, including flowers, limousines, a videographer, the rehearsal dinner, and the reception. Set your priorities; adjust your budget around the categories you consider most important.

BUDGET CATEGORIES

The following checklist includes traditional costs associated with a wedding. Some are mandatory, such as marriage license fees, and some are optional, such as limousines and a videographer. Whether an optional category is mandatory to you is *your* decision.

WEDDING BUDGET	MANDATORY/ OPTIONAL	COST (ESTIMATED)	COST (ACTUAL)
ATTENDANTS			
ACCOMMODATIONS			
BRIDESMAIDS LUNCHEON			
TIES AND GLOVES			
SUBTOTAL			
CEREMONY FEES			
OFFICIANT'S FEE			
CHURCH OR SYNAGOGUE FEE			
ORGANIST'S FEE			
CANTOR/VOCALIST/ INSTRUMENTALIST FEE(S)			
SEXTON'S FEE			
AWNING/AISLE CARPET RENTAL			
SUBTOTAL			
FLOWERS			
CEREMONY			
RECEPTION			
BRIDAL BOUQUET			
BRIDAL ATTENDANTS' FLOWERS			
CORSAGES			
BOUTONNIERES			
SUBTOTAL			
GIFTS			
BRIDE'S GIFTS FOR ATTENDANTS			
GROOM'S GIFTS FOR ATTENDANTS			
BRIDE'S GIFT FOR GROOM			
GROOM'S GIFT FOR BRIDE			
HONEYMOON COSTS			
SUBTOTAL			
LEGALITIES			
MARRIAGE LICENSE			
HEALTH/PHYSICAL/BLOOD TEST FEES			

(CONTINUED)

WEDDING BUDGET (CONT.)	MANDATORY/ OPTIONAL	COST (ESTIMATED)	COST (ACTUAL)
MUSIC FOR RECEPTION			
SUBTOTAL			
PHOTOGRAPHY			
ENGAGEMENT PHOTOGRAPHS			
PHOTOGRAPHER			
VIDEOGRAPHER			
SUBTOTAL			
PRINTED MATERIALS			
ANNOUNCEMENTS			
STATIONERY FOR THANK-YOU NOTES			
CALLIGRAPHY			
POSTAGE			
CEREMONY PROGRAM			
SUBTOTAL			
RECEPTION			
SITE RENTAL/SETUP			
SITE DECORATIONS			
FOOD/BEVERAGE EXPENSES (PER-PERSON COST)			
RECEPTION FAVORS (PER-PERSON COST)			
WEDDING CAKE			
SUBTOTAL			
TRANSPORTATION/PARKING			
LIMOUSINES FOR BRIDAL PARTY			
TRAFFIC OFFICIALS AT CEREMONY AT, RECEPTION			
VALET PARKING			
TRAVEL COSTS FOR CEREMONY OFFICIANT, IF NECESSARY			
TRIPS HOME DURING PLANNING IF YOU LIVE AWAY			
SUBTOTAL			

(CONTINUED)

Expenses

WEDDING BUDGET (CONT.)	MANDATORY/ OPTIONAL	COST (ESTIMATED)	COST (ACTUAL)
WEDDING ATTIRE			
BRIDAL GOWN			
BRIDAL ACCESSORIES			
GROOM'S OUTFIT			
BRIDE'S RINGS			
GROOM'S RING			
BEAUTY COSTS (HAIR, NAILS, MAKEUP)			
SUBTOTAL			
WEDDING CONSULTANT FEES			
SUBTOTAL			
MISCELLANEOUS:			
TELEPHONE BILLS RELATED TO PLANNING			
WARDROBE COSTS FOR WEDDING-RELATED EVENTS			
TIPS (IF NOT INCLUDED IN ABOVE COSTS)			
TAXES (IF NOT INCLUDED IN ABOVE COSTS)			
NONFLORAL CHURCH DECORATION			
SUBTOTAL			
TOTAL			

HOW MUCH TO TIP

Percentages vary regionally, with the highest in major cities.
Following is a general guide for tipping:

CATEGORY	HOW MUCH	HOW TO TIP
WAITERS/WAITRESSES	15–20% OF FOOD AND DRINK BILL	*if not included in final bill, give to table captain or banquet manager to distribute*
BARTENDERS	15–20% OF DRINK BILL	*if not included in final bill, give to banquet manager to divide and distribute among bartenders*
TABLE CAPTAINS	15–20% OF FOOD AND DRINK BILL	*if not included in final bill, give to banquet manager to divide and distribute among bartenders*
POWDER ROOM ATTENDANT	FLAT FEE OR 50 CENTS TO $1 PER GUEST	*make arrangements to include in final bill, either flat fee or amount per guest; have manager distribute just before or after reception*
COAT-CHECK ATTENDANT, VALET PARKING	FLAT FEE OR $1 PER GUEST FOR EACH SERVICE	*if not in contract or bill, distribute just before reception or have manager distribute among attendants at each station*

TIPS ON TIPPING

Many wedding professionals, from bridal consultants to photographers, are tipped only for extra-special service. If your florist arrived to decorate the ceremony site only to find a locked door, which caused him to wait an extra hour, a tip would be an extra thank-you for his professionalism, patience, and diligence. While you might set aside an extra 15 percent as an unexpected tip fund, you needn't anticipate tips for the consultant, club manager or caterer, florist, photographer or videographer. Often a caterer's gratuities are included in the total costs; many hotels include a service charge for the wait staff. Always ask whether gratuities are included before signing any contract.

You should plan a gratuity budget for the following in case gratuities are not included in the overall contracts and bills for their services:

- Valet Parking
- Coat Check
- Powder Room Attendants
- Wait Staff
- Bartenders
- Table Captains

BEFORE YOU SIGN A CONTRACT

You should expect to sign a contract with every supplier, from the stationer to the florist to the limousine service to the wedding consultant. *Every single detail* should be covered in writing in the contract, including taxes, gratuities, dates, delivery schedules, payment plans, cancellation fees, and refund policies. Take the time to read everything thoroughly; if you don't understand something, ask questions until you do. Be sure you are clear on how and when bills are to be paid—and make sure there are clauses in the contract that ensure proper restitution in the event of a snafu that is clearly the vendor's responsibility.

Staple your copy of each contract to the appropriate section of your wedding planner or keep contacts together in a notebook or file that travels with you. You never know when you are going to need to confirm a detail or check an arrangement.

SAVING ON A DESTINATION WEDDING

If your dream is to be married at a popular travel spot, plan early to ensure availability, and give yourself plenty of time to shop around for the best prices. Or have a professional do the work for you. You'll be ahead of the game—and will likely save money in the long run—when you enlist the services of the professionals below:

- Find a travel agent who specializes in destination weddings and related components—finding officiants, florists, bands, photographers, and caterers. You'll want an agent who will spend the time to find the best airline rates and who can advise you on the difference between in-season and out-of-season costs at your destination, since the price differences can often be considerable.
- Find a wedding consultant who has experience in planning destination weddings, and let him or her make the arrangements for you. Provide a detailed list of your preferences.
- Locate an on-site resort planner, and let him or her take care of contracting the services you will need. You'll be spared the time spent doing the legwork, the long-distance calls, and any difficulty in communicating in another language.

BUDGET FOR THE HONEYMOON

In the frenzy of planning and budgeting, couples often forget that honeymoon costs are greater than just those of transportation and lodging. Be sure to include moneys in your planning budget for the following.

MEALS _____

TRANSFERS _____

TIPS* _____

TAXES _____

SOUVENIRS _____

LITTLE LUXURIES

    (MASSAGES, POOLSIDE LOUNGE CHAIRS

    AND TOWELS) _____

SIGHTSEEING TICKETS AND FEES _____

    SPORTS-RELATED FEES

    (BIKE RENTALS, SNORKELING

    OUTINGS, TENNIS COURT FEES,

    GOLF COURSE FEES, LESSONS) _____

NIGHTCLUB/ENTERTAINMENT FEES _____

TOTAL _____

* On a cruise, for example, any number of attendants will expect tips.
In many European countries, an automatic 15 to 20 percent gratuity is added
to the bill, making additional tipping unnecessary. Look for phrases such as
"servis compris" and "servizio compreso," which both translate to
"service included."

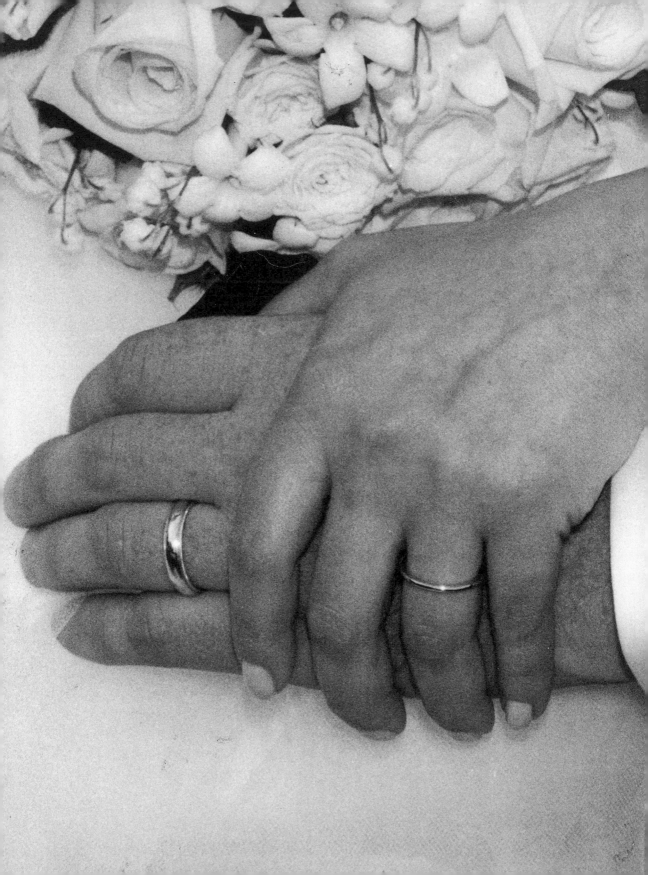

CHAPTER 4

LEGALITIES AND
OTHER MATTERS

In order to be married, you must live up to the letter of the law; the law varies, not just from country to country but from state to state and even from city to city as well. In some regions, a designated length-of-residency is stipulated; in others, specific medical tests are required. Some regions require both. The bottom line: Research the laws and regulations at your wedding location well in advance of the ceremony so that, come your wedding day, all will be legal and above board.

LEGALITIES:
PLANNING AT A GLANCE

❏ Investigate the legal requirements of acquiring a marriage license in the locale of your ceremony. SHORTLY AFTER BECOMING ENGAGED

❏ Apply for and obtain the license. VARIES, DEPENDING ON THE STATE (OR COUNTRY, IN CASE OF DESTINATION WEDDINGS); USUALLY BETWEEN 24 HOURS AND 60 DAYS IN ADVANCE

❏ Make sure all your requirements are covered and in writing on any contracts you have with vendors (reception site, florist, photographer, caterer). AT TIME BOOKINGS ARE MADE

❏ Discuss and draw up any prenuptial agreements with lawyers, then each other. GENERALLY ONE TO SIX MONTHS IN ADVANCE

❏ Have blood work and any other medical tests done, as required. VARIES FROM LOCATION TO LOCATION

❏ Apply for or renew passport, if necessary. THREE TO FOUR MONTHS IN ADVANCE

❏ Plan any financial changes. START TWO TO THREE MONTHS IN ADVANCE

❏ Notify banks, employers, and other agencies and organizations of name and/or address changes. START ONE TO TWO MONTHS IN ADVANCE; FINALIZE AS APPROPRIATE

GETTING MARRIED IN THE U.S.A.: THE BASICS

MARRIAGE LICENSE AND MARRIAGE CERTIFICATE

A marriage license authorizes you to get married. A marriage certificate is the document that proves you are married and is issued by the county office where you were married, usually within a few weeks after the ceremony.

- In general, a marriage license may only be used in the state where it is obtained, and then within a certain period of time, usually between 24 hours and 60 days, depending on the state; otherwise, the license expires.
- Some states require a three-day waiting period from the time applicants apply for a license to the time the license is issued.
- Those states with the strictest requirements strongly advise that the bride and groom obtain their marriage license two to three weeks before their wedding day.

ARE SAME-SEX WEDDINGS LEGAL?

Generally, couples must be of the opposite sex to form a valid marriage. Religions have their own gender regulations, but there is a growing trend among clergy to bless same-sex unions. Most states do not allow same-sex marriages, but in Hawaii, Alaska, and Vermont, arguments are being made in the courts that a marriage license cannot be denied based on the sex of the applicants. On the other hand, some states, including Georgia, South Dakota, Texas, and Utah, have passed laws designed to thwart same-sex marriages. Indeed, in 1996 the Defense of Marriage Act became U.S. law, barring the federal government from recognizing same-sex marriages and permitting states to ignore same-sex marriages performed in other states.

Even though most states do not recognize same-sex marriages, many agencies and companies are adopting "domestic partnership" policies that accept same-sex relationships. Policies range from fair housing regulations to the granting of traditional marital benefits, such as insurance coverage, family leave, and bereavement leave.

LEGALITIES SHORTCUTS

I f you don't relish the thought of waiting in line at places such as the Department of Motor Vehicles to report a name change, let The Wedding Helpers give you a head start. The company offers a Name Change Kit that contains forms from all the local and federal government agencies you need to notify of a name change, as well as sample letters to banks, doctors, and the like. (The Wedding Helpers, Name Change Kit, 800–274–0675; $29.95)

MARRIAGE LICENSE APPLICATION CHECKLIST

In general, each of you should have on hand the following information when you apply for a marriage license.

❑ Full name of the contracting party (bride or groom) _____

_____

❑ Place of birth _____

❑ Age and date of birth _____

❑ Civil status _____

❑ Documentation showing end of previous marriage, if applicable_____

❑ Present residence and citizenship_____

_____

❑ Full name, residence, and citizenship of the father _____

_____

❑ Full name, residence, and citizenship of the mother _____

_____

❑ Full name, residence, and citizenship of the guardian or person having charge, in the event that the contracting party has neither father nor mother and is under the age of 18 years _____

_____

_____

Proof of Age

In most of the United States, you must be of a certain age to legally marry. Generally:

- If either applicant is under 14 years of age, a marriage license cannot be issued.
- If either applicant is 14 or 15 years of age, he or she must present the written approval and consent of a justice of the Supreme Court or a judge of the Family Court who has jurisdiction over the town or city in which the application is made.
- If either applicant is 16 or 17 years of age, he or she must present the written consent of both of his or her parents.
- If both applicants are 18 years of age or older, no parental or legal consent, regarding age, is required.

No one may legally take your word for it that you are actually the age you say you are. In most states, you may be required to submit documentary proof of age. Generally, one or more of the following documents showing proof of age is required and acceptable:

- Birth Certificate
- Baptismal Record
- Passport
- Driver's License
- Life Insurance Policy
- Employment Certificate
- School Record
- Immigration Record
- Naturalization Record
- Court Record

Medical Tests

- Many states require that persons planning to be married have blood tests and be examined and found free of venereal disease and rubella before they can legally wed.
- Some health certificates have time restrictions. For example, you may obtain the certificate from a private physician or health department, but it may only be good for 60 days from the date of the examination.

RELIGIOUS REQUIREMENTS

Some religions also have rules and regulations that must be adhered to. If it is important to you to be married by a priest, rabbi, or minister or in a church, temple, or synagogue, you will need to know the requirements beforehand. Find out those requirements as soon as possible from your officiant. Requirements may include:

- Premarital counseling sessions
- Membership in the religious faith and place of worship
- Banns (a public statement of intent to marry that asks anyone who may object to do so; published over a three-week period)
- Special regulations for people who have been divorced

WITNESSES

Some states require that a witness, in addition to an authorized member of the clergy or pubic official, must be present during the wedding ceremony. In some of these states, there is no minimum age for a witness, but it is suggested that he or she be deemed competent enough to testify in a court proceeding regarding what was witnessed.

LEGALITIES FOR REMARRIAGES

When applying for a marriage license, those who have been married before must provide information regarding previous marriages. The information the applicant needs to provide includes, but may not be restricted to, the following.

- A copy of the Decree of Divorce or a Certificate of Dissolution of Marriage or a death certificate of previous spouse (be sure to bring the original document or a certified copy).
- Month, day, and year of final divorce decree _____
- County and state where divorce was granted _____
- Grounds for divorce _____
- Whether former spouse or spouses are living _____

DESTINATION WEDDINGS: THE LEGALITIES OF MARRYING IN OTHER COUNTRIES

Every country in the world has a different set of legal requirements for tying the knot. Some ask for residency requirements of a certain duration. Others require a specific number of witnesses. Still others require specific documentation. Marriages that are legally performed and valid abroad generally are also legally valid in the United States.

Here are some tips for U.S. citizens who wish to marry in another country:

- Write or telephone the country's U.S.–based consulate or tourist office to learn what requirements and documentation you need to legally wed there. The office can provide specific instructions over the phone, by mail, or by fax. Tourist offices can also be found on the Internet.
- You can also receive general information on marrying abroad by contacting the Office of Citizens Consular Services (Room 4817, Dept. of State, Washington, DC 20520).
- In some cases the town you plan to marry in has its own requirements separate from the country's legalities. In Mexico, for example, the requirements vary from town to town, so once you've gotten the basic information from the tourist office, you will need to call the registrar's office in the town where you plan to get married.
- Have an on-site wedding planner or travel agent do the legwork for you. Many resorts offer total packages that include obtaining the marriage

VIVA LAS VEGAS!

The Las Vegas wedding is synonymous with fast and easy—and for good reason. The legal requirements are minimal. You don't need blood tests, there is no waiting period, and license fees are a low $35. In addition, the Marriage License Bureau is open seven days a week, from 8 A.M. until midnight Mondays through Thursdays, and 24 hours a day on weekends and holidays. If you've been divorced, you need only provide the date of the final decree and the city and state where it was issued. Check out the Las Vegas/Clark County wedding website at www.co.clark.NV.US for more information.

license. Travel agencies that specialize in wedding planning can provide information on the documentation required and what restrictions apply.

- If you're marrying in another country, don't forget to check on your legal and religious requirements at home as well. Check your passport, medical requirements, and documentation needed for ensuring the validity of your marriage in the United States.
- You can get around the legal requirements of marrying abroad by being wed on a U.S. military base, which is under U.S. jurisdiction.

NAME, ADDRESS, AND FINANCIAL CHANGES

NAME AND ADDRESS CHANGES: WHO TO NOTIFY

There are many options for brides today. The most popular choices are: the bride takes her husband's last name; retains her own surname; or hyphenates both her own surname and her husband's surname. The name change occurs simply by entering the new name in the appropriate space provided on the marriage license.

If you plan to change your name in any form, you must notify several people, companies, agencies, and organizations, including the following:

- ❏ Social Security Administration
- ❏ Motor Vehicles Department
- ❏ Passport Agency
- ❏ Employer Payroll Department
- ❏ Banks
- ❏ Credit Unions
- ❏ Mortgage Company
- ❏ Credit Card Companies
- ❏ Voter Registration
- ❏ Religious Organizations
- ❏ School Alumni Organizations
- ❏ Magazine Subscriptions
- ❏ Credit Accounts (Local Stores)
- ❏ Frequent Traveler Clubs
- ❏ Financial Planner (or Investment Firms/Stock Broker)
- ❏ Doctors and Dentists

EIGHT INTERNATIONAL WEDDING DESTINATIONS: LEGAL REQUIREMENTS

ARUBA

- Both of you need to bring a valid U.S. passport or a birth certificate and a picture I.D.
- There is no waiting period for a marriage license approval. Pick up the license at the Office of Legal Affairs. The office is open on weekdays (check times) but not on weekends. Get there early on Friday; the office closes at 3 P.M.

THE BAHAMAS

- One member of the couple must have resided in the islands of the Bahamas for no less than 24 hours prior to the date of the application, and both parties must be present at the time of the application.
- A declaration certifying United States citizenship must be sworn before a United States Consul at the American Embassy.
- Regardless of country of origin, both the bride and groom must produce a photo I.D., issued by a government office in the country where both reside.

BRITISH VIRGIN ISLANDS

- A three-day residency in the British Virgin Islands is required.
- To obtain a marriage license on one of the islands, Tortola, you will need to go to the Registrar's Office and show a valid passport or birth certificate, a photo I.D., and—if you've been married before—a divorce decree or a death certificate of previous spouse.

FIJI

- Provide a birth certificate as proof of identity and, if you have been divorced or widowed, your original divorce decree or previous spouse's death certificate.
- Once you arrive, simply pick up your license at the Registrar's Office (open weekdays only).

FRANCE/FRENCH WEST INDIES

- One member of the couple needs to live in the country or on one of the country's islands at least 40 days prior to the wedding in order to get a proof of residency.
- You will need a birth certificate or passport and, if you have been divorced or widowed, your original divorce decree or previous spouse's death certificate.

GREECE

- Foreign nationals in Greece may be married either in a civil ceremony by a mayor, in a religious ceremony by a priest, or both.
- Although there is no residency requirement for foreign nationals wishing to marry in Greece, the bureaucratic procedure may take several weeks to complete before a certificate from the U.S. Consulate in Greece stating that there is no impediment to the marriage may be obtained.
- A valid U.S. marriage license from one's current place of residence, prior to coming to Greece, is generally accepted by the Greek authorities—as long as neither the bride nor the groom is a resident in Greece and provided that the license does not contain statements restricting them from accepting it.
- You may decide to obtain a marriage license in Greece instead, after showing required documents.

ITALY

- You and your intended, along with four unrelated friends, need to visit the Italian consulate in the U.S. Bring along a certified copy of your birth certificate with the Apostille seal. Your friends then sign an affidavit stating that they know you and that you are free to marry.
- Once in Italy, you and your intended go to the U.S. consulate nearest your wedding site to sign a second affidavit much like the first.
- Once in Italy, obtain your license in any local city hall.

MEXICO

- You will need a certified copy of both your birth certificates or valid passports and a copy of your visas or tourist cards.
- Cities have varying requirements for medical tests, so check with local authorities. Generally, blood tests are required within 15 days of your wedding date.
- You will need four witnesses. In some cities, the law requires witnesses to be Mexican; other cities permit witnesses to be U.S. citizens.
- The wedding party must spend two to four days in Mexico prior to the wedding to complete certain pre-wedding requirements, which vary from county to county and town to town.
- If you have been divorced or widowed, you will need a certified copy of the divorce decree or death certificate as well as verification that a minimum period of one year has elapsed since the divorce or death occurred.

The engaged couple should discuss financial considerations to determine how finances will be handled after marriage. Issues to discuss include,

- **BANK ACCOUNTS**. Checking and savings accounts: joint or separate?
- **WILLS**. When there is no pre- or post-nuptial contract, the bride and groom would be smart to put their wills and finances in order so that the disposition of their money and property is clear to each other or, should both die, to their families.
- **INSURANCE BENEFICIARIES**. Decide whether to make any change on existing insurance policies—such as life, health, and homeowner's—or change beneficiaries on retirement plan payouts. Assuming you want to make each other the beneficiary on any existing policies you own, you should call an insurance broker and talk to your human resources head at work to see what is required to make these changes.
- **FEDERAL AND STATE TAX RAMIFICATIONS OF MARRIAGE**. Contact your employer to adjust your federal and state deductions as necessary.
- **BILL-PAYING RESPONSIBILITIES**.

MARRYING SOMEONE WHO IS A CITIZEN OF ANOTHER COUNTRY

Marriage by an American to a foreign national requires its own set of documents and qualifications, including certified English translation of any required documentation. You can get information on obtaining a visa for a foreign spouse from any office of the Immigration and Naturalization Service, U.S. embassies and consulates abroad, or the U.S. Department of State Visa Office.

PRENUPTIAL AGREEMENTS

A premarital agreement is a contract between two people that defines the rights and benefits that will exist during the marriage and after, in the event of divorce or death. Without a premarital agreement, state laws define the rights and benefits of marriage. A prenuptial agreement must be in writing to be legally binding. The bride and groom should each retain a lawyer to prepare his or her portion of the agreement. Some frequently asked questions about prenuptial agreements include,

1. *What can a prenuptial agreement do?*
   - It can expand or limit a person's right to property, life insurance benefits, or support payments in the event of death or divorce.
   - Usually, it addresses the rights to property that each brings to the marriage, retirement plan assets, and how money accumulated before the marriage will be distributed in the event of death or divorce.

2. *When is it used?*
   - A prenuptial agreement is most often used when the bride or the groom or both bring assets to the marriage that they want to protect in the event of divorce. This is particularly true for people marrying for the second or third time who want to make sure that certain assets are passed on to their children from a previous marriage.

3. *What does a prenuptial contract not cover?*
   - Child custody and support. The courts will disregard the contract on this point and make a decision that is considered in the best interest of the child.
   - The courts will also disregard a premarital agreement that, in essence, leaves one person destitute.

4. *When is a post-nuptial contract made?*
   - A post-nuptial contract is one made after a couple is married and can include the same categories of consideration—usually having to do with property and money—in a prenuptial contract. This contract is usually drawn up if the couple realizes that children from a previous marriage or other family members would be unprotected in the case of divorce or death.

5. How can one broach the subject of a premarital agreement diplomatically?

- It is often as difficult for those requesting a premarital contract to broach the subject as it is being asked to sign one. Again, a prenuptial contract may simply be a way of protecting assets you bring into the marriage in the unlikely event of divorce or death. A couple that communicates well has a head start in discussing a prenuptial contract. If you are the person requesting a premarital agreement, do so with tact, love, and honesty. Explain exactly why you are making the request and whether it affects the assets you amass as a couple (it shouldn't). Discuss the lifetime of assets you hope to build together as a couple, assets completely separate from the assets protected in the prenuptial agreement.

WEDDING INSURANCE

Wedding insurance may be taken out by a bride and groom to cover wedding catastrophes that are beyond anyone's control. Wedding insurance can be obtained from the Fireman's Fund insurance company (800–ENGAGED). In some instances, the cost of a wedding is so astronomical that the additional cost of insurance is worth every penny if it protects such a large investment. Possible wedding catastrophes include:

- Any retaking of photographs, replacements of lost or damaged wedding attire or wedding gifts, and public liability.
- When, for example, a reception site suddenly cannot accommodate the party for reasons including fire, damage, a murder or suicide occurring at the site, or an outbreak of a contagious disease requiring a health department quarantine. Insurance will cover the cost of rebooking elsewhere.
- When the reception site is suddenly not available and the wedding must be canceled because no other site is available on such short notice, resulting in the loss of other costs, such as formal-wear rental, car hire, hotel charges for the wedding party, and flower arrangements.

WHO CAN PERFORM THE CEREMONY?

A list of persons specified by law as authorized to perform a marriage ceremony is defined within the Domestic Relations Law of each state. The following is a general list of those who can perform a marriage ceremony.

1. *Religious ceremonies:*
   - A member of the clergy (i.e., priest, rabbi, bishop, iman, or minister) who has been officially ordained and granted authority to perform marriage ceremonies from a governing religious body in accordance with the rules and regulations of that faith
   - A member of the clergy or minister who is not authorized by a governing church body but who has been chosen by a spiritual group to preside over their spiritual affairs
   - A tribal chief (for Native American weddings).

2. *Nonreligious ceremonies (also called civil ceremonies):*
   - The mayor of a city or village
   - The city clerk or one of the deputy city clerks of a city with over one million inhabitants
   - A marriage officer appointed by the town or village board or the city common council
   - A justice or judge in most courts
   - A village, town, or county justice
   - A court clerk who has legal authority to perform marriages
   - A person given temporary authority by a judge or court clerk to conduct a marriage ceremony.

3. *A short list of those who may not perform the ceremony:*
   - Contrary to popular belief, ship captains often will not perform or are not universally authorized to perform marriage ceremonies. Increasingly, however, cruise lines are working out ways for legally recognized marriages to be performed aboard ship by ship captains.
   - Consulate heads and diplomats.

Legalities and Other Matters

Ms. Katharvie Wilheim

8

Miss Sharada Strasmore

9

Ms. Emily Wilheim

CHAPTER 5

GUESTS AND GUEST LISTS

A guest list is the biggest factor in the cost of a wedding. That's because reception costs generally are the most expensive aspect of weddings today. Most brides and grooms, in planning their nuptials, find they must work around financial considerations—and paring a guest list is often the best way to cut costs. Still, guest lists have a way of multiplying at a surprising rate. You and your intended will have to decide whether you want to plan your guest list and reception around a budget or make a guest list first and plan the reception around that. Either way, with two sets of families weighing in on invitation decisions, you will likely find yourself relying on a good measure of tact and diplomacy as you tinker with and fine-tune your guest list.

THE GUEST LIST

The size of the guest list is dependent on several factors and is chosen based on the following. Use these considerations to arrive at a reasonable estimate.

- The size of your ceremony and reception sites
- The level of intimacy desired for the wedding
- Your wedding budget
- The lists made up by the families of the bride and groom
- Whether you plan to include children
- Whether you plan for single friends to bring guests

MAKING A LIST, CHECKING IT TWICE

Cutting down an overambitious guest list is a difficult task requiring great tact, diplomacy, and even-handedness. Approach the task methodically by doing the following:

- Traditionally each family is allotted half of the desired total guest count, a figure largely determined by the person hosting the wedding. Then the list is often divided into quarters, with the bride's family, the groom's family, the bride, and the groom all getting to invite a quarter of the guests. Today, the percentages might vary greatly, depending on many variables (the location of the wedding, who is paying, whether the wedding is the first one for the bride and groom).
- First ask each half (or one-fourth) to compile a rough list of "must-have" guests, supplemented by "hopefuls" to be invited if there should be room. (Remember to include in your count the officiant and his or her spouse, yourselves, both sets of parents, and your wedding party.)
- Try to redraw your lines equilaterally, bumping entire groupings of people—second cousins, work associates with whom you've never socialized, friends from the health club—to a "B" List. These people can be invited four weeks before the wedding if guests on the "A" List send regrets. This guide should be based on what makes sense in your case. Any planning must be adapted to your situation. Your list may read something like this:

1 ST TIER: immediate families (parents, siblings, grandparents, the couple's own children)

2 ND TIER: extended family members (aunts, uncles, cousins, nieces, nephews)

3 RD TIER: family friends (parents' close friends, long-time friends and neighbors, childhood friends and their parents, if close to you)

4 TH TIER: bride and groom's friends, in progressive tiers of closeness to you (childhood friends, high school and college friends, work friends, new friends)

5 TH TIER: parents' colleagues (associates, employers, employees)

DON'T FORGET

Don't forget to send invitations to all the members of the bridal party to have as keepsakes. And don't forget to add their names to your guest list when giving a final head count to the caterer or club manager for the reception.

A Tier of Their Own

A few special guests do not fit into any of the priority tiers but should be included on the guest list. Check each off when you have invited him or her.

- ❏ The person who performs the ceremony and his or her spouse (necessary)

  _____

- ❏ The parents of ring bearers and flower girls (necessary) _____
- ❏ The parents of the bridesmaids (not necessary, but a nice gesture when feasible, especially when the bride knows them well) _____
- ❏ Counselors, advisors, or mentors to the bride or groom who are not close friends but who have been an important part of their lives (not absolutely necessary but often meaningful) _____

THE FINAL LIST

The master guest list is the foundation of your wedding plans and as such should be carefully maintained. Use the Guest List at the back of this planner (on page 260) to keep your list.

Standby Guest List

Before the master-list invitations are even mailed, ask everyone involved in creating the guest list for the names and addresses of "wait list" guests; then you and your partner can prioritize them. Although some couples are hesitant to have standby lists, they do provide a practical solution for controlling the numbers—and budget. Following are some pointers on standby guest lists.

- Make sure you plan for enough time for responses from master-list guests to be received—no less than four weeks—to invite guests who are on the standby list.
- Once guests from the standby invitation list accept, incorporate their names into the master list in your wedding organizer.
- Be discreet: Make sure that guests have no inkling that "A" and "B" Lists exist. Keep the list separate from the Planner. If the guests on that list receive an invitation, simply write their names and other information on your master list.

WEDDING ANNOUNCEMENT LIST

If wedding announcements are to be mailed after the wedding, put together a list of the names and addresses of people who will be receiving your announcements so that you can order the announcements well in advance. This way, you can address and stamp them in advance, and arrange for a friend or relative to mail them on the day or next few days after the wedding. In fact, perhaps you can even ask your friend to take care of addressing the announcements for you, too.

WELCOME BASKETS FOR OUT-OF-TOWNERS

Have your florist or party planner prepare welcome baskets to greet out-of-town guests when they check into their hotel room. (This is also something you and your attendants could do together—have a Welcome Basket party!)

Include ESSENTIAL INFORMATION...

- a schedule of activities and festivities
- transportation arrangements
- maps
- brochures or lists of local places of interest and activities
- SPECIAL INDULGENCES:
  - a bottle of wine or champagne
  - a pass to the hotel spa
  - fresh flowers
  - chocolates
  - souvenirs
  - tiny toiletry bottles containing shampoo, lotion, aromatic soap, and oils
  - aromatic candles

WEDDING ANNOUNCEMENT LIST

Photocopy this page as necessary to compile your list.

FULL NAME _____

ADDRESS _____

RELATIONSHIP _____

FULL NAME _____

ADDRESS _____

RELATIONSHIP _____

FULL NAME _____

ADDRESS _____

RELATIONSHIP _____

FULL NAME _____

ADDRESS _____

RELATIONSHIP _____

FULL NAME _____

ADDRESS _____

RELATIONSHIP _____

FULL NAME _____

ADDRESS _____

RELATIONSHIP _____

FULL NAME _____

ADDRESS _____

RELATIONSHIP _____

FULL NAME _____

ADDRESS _____

RELATIONSHIP _____

Guests and
Guest Lists

HELP! WHAT DO I DO ABOUT. . .

1. . . . **INVITING CHILDREN?** If space, time of day, limited finances, or simply concern about having little ones at your reception is an issue, you may have to draw the line when it comes to inviting children. You can approach this in a number of different ways: You may decide to include family members only, children of a certain age, or no children at all. It is inappropriate to write "No Children" on the invitations. Instead, communicate your wishes by leaving children's names off the invitations—write only the parents' names on the inner and outer envelopes—or through word-of-mouth. You might also want to personally tell certain relatives or friends about your plans for no children. An additional courtesy: hiring a baby-sitter during the hours of the wedding celebrations to watch children of out-of-town guests, either at a friend or relative's home or at the hotel where the guests are staying.

2. . . . **INVITING PARTNERS?** Partners of invited guests must be included in a wedding invitation, whether they are married, engaged, or living together and whether anyone in the wedding party knows them. A nice touch (although optional) is to suggest that single guests who aren't attached to a significant other bring a date.

   A single invitation addressed to both members of a couple who live together is sent to their shared address, while invitations to an engaged or long-standing couple who don't live together are sent separately to each address. Envelopes addressed to a single friend may include "and Guest," indicating that he or she may bring an escort or friend. If it is possible to obtain the name of the guest, the name would be included on the invitation to the friend. Or a second invitation may be sent directly to the date at his or her home address instead.

3. . . . **GUESTS WHO ASK TO BRING A GUEST?** It is impolite for a guest to ask if he or she can bring a date—but it is not impolite for you to refuse. You may certainly answer no. If you do discover, however, that they are engaged or living together, the thing to do is invite your friend's partner.

4. . . . **INVITATIONS TO OUT-OF-TOWN GUESTS WHO CAN'T POSSIBLY ATTEND?** Many people prefer not to send invitations to those friends and acquaintances whom they think cannot possibly attend the celebrations. In most cases, these friends should receive a wedding announcement instead, which carries no gift obligation whatsoever.

   There is the flip side to this dilemma. Some good friends who live far away might actually be hurt if you don't invite them, even if your intent was to spare them from feeling obliged to send a gift for a wedding so far away. These friends, having heard the news of your engagement, may actually have been planning to travel to your wedding. In general, invite good friends— even if they live far away.

OUT-OF-TOWN GUESTS

Planning entertainment for out-of-town guests who are not part of the wedding party has become yet another consideration of wedding planning. Although you are certainly not obligated to do so, it is a nice touch to offer activities, gatherings, and other forms of hospitality to those who have come from far away to celebrate your nuptials. Also, you might be approached by friends and relatives offering to help out or to host a gathering or meal for out-of-town guests. In some cases, the costs and preparations are shared by a group of friends and family. Keep the following in mind when you or friends and relatives entertain out-of-town guests:

- You will need to provide the hosts of these parties with a list of names and addresses so that they can send invitations, if necessary, and plan their party accordingly. You can get a good idea of the number of out-of-town guests by referring to your master guest list (in the space to check whether a guest is from out of town).
- If out-of-town guests are staying in private homes, their hosts should be invited to the events or parties as well. Thus, be sure to provide the party hosts with the names and addresses of those who are providing accommodations.
- Don't forget to send thank-you gifts or flowers to the party hosts, plus your words of appreciation.
- The best times for entertaining out-of-town guests may include the following:

  1. During the rehearsal dinner
  2. On the day of an evening wedding
  3. At a post-wedding brunch

LODGING FOR OUT-OF-TOWN GUESTS

Out-of-town guests are expected to pay for their own lodging; the exception is if they are members of the bridal party. Bridal-party members are expected to pay for any extra hotel charges (such as movie rentals, room service, health club fees) when they check out. Following are some ideas for helping out-of-town guests find places to stay:

- Pre-reserve, on behalf of your guests, a block of rooms in a hotel; if a minimum number of rooms is booked, you may even get discount room rates for your guests. Have guests make their reservations as early as possible. A nice touch: Greet guests at check-in with a welcome note, and possibly include another copy of a map to the ceremony and a list of other out-of-town guests.
- Some friends might offer to put up out-of-town guests at their homes. Make sure that all involved are comfortable with the arrangement and that the hosts and the guests are a good match. Then either you or the hosts can send the out-of-town guests the names and addresses of their host and hostess and directions to their home, letting them know what to expect (whether their hosts have a pet, a swimming pool, children, and the like). Make sure the hosts are clear on the guests' arrival and departure times. Remember to give a thank-you gift to those who are providing lodging.

ACTIVITIES FOR OUT-OF-TOWN GUESTS

If there is open time in the wedding-celebrations schedule, you may want to provide your out-of-town guests with a list of local activities, sports centers, museums, and other attractions, along with addresses and phone numbers. Here's where you can get creative: Your town may have a singular attraction that's a must-see for any person new to the area; you might even provide tickets or passes. Don't make an activity mandatory, however—simply provide enticing options. You might ask a friend to gather local information for you to give to out-of-town guests.

WHEN KIDS ARE GUESTS

If you are planning to invite a number of children to your wedding celebrations, you'll want to make sure that your menu includes some kid-friendly foods. Many couples find that coming up with ways to keep kids occupied can be great fun. Consider the following:

- Have your floral designer create a piñata, filled with inexpensive toys.
- Set up a designated children's table with coloring books and favors. If children are seated with parents, you could still provide each with a coloring book and a small box of crayons.
- If you are having an outdoor wedding, you can set up a badminton net or have a puppet show.
- If your reception includes dancing, you might encourage the kids to join in.
- Hire a baby-sitter or two to help out. Some reception sites even provide a separate room where children can color, watch a video, or just gather. In that case, the kids should be supervised, and baby-sitters are a must.

MARY-ELIZABETH TONDREAU
and
PATRICK JAMES O'NEILL
request the honor of your presence
at their wedding on
Saturday, May 8th, 1993
at three o'clock
St. Paul's Chapel
Columbia University
New York, NY

PLEASE ENTER THROUGH
THE MAIN GATE AT
116TH STREET &
BROADWAY

CHAPTER 6

INVITATIONS AND OTHER PRINTED ACCESSORIES

A wedding invitation should convey not only essential practical information—the who, what, when, and where of the nuptial proceedings—but also a sense of the style and formality of the celebration planned. It's a reflection of your personal tastes as well—and often a subtle indicator of your preferences in wedding gifts and pre-wedding celebrations. For many couples, the wedding invitation is also a keepsake to preserve for display, whether in a picture frame or affixed to marble.

It's a good idea to start shopping around for invitations as soon as your wedding date is firmly set. The process of choosing, ordering, preparing related enclosures for, addressing, and mailing the invitations is not easily compressed. The rule of thumb: allow at least six to eight weeks for the printing of formal invitations and their related enclosures. Similarly, factor in two to four weeks to address envelopes, whether you have hired a calligrapher or will be doing it yourself. Plan to address your invitations no later than two months before the wedding and mail them six to eight weeks before the wedding date.

When the decision to marry is an impromptu one, time-pressed couples may telephone, fax, or overnight-mail their invitations to family and close friends.

CHOOSING INVITATIONS: WHAT'S YOUR STYLE?

The first step in shopping for invitations is to choose a basic style: whether you decide on third-person formal, semiformal, or in the case of an intimate wedding, handwritten notes on beautiful stationery. While this decision is largely a matter of personal style, you should consider the degree of formality you want the invitation to convey. If there is an underlying color, floral, or seasonal theme

INVITATIONS: PLANNING AT A GLANCE

❏ Begin researching options for invitations, related enclosures, announcements, and other stationery needs. Obtain samples. Compare costs. Check the background of unfamiliar printers or stationers.

ABOUT SIX TO EIGHT MONTHS IN ADVANCE

❏ Determine your preferences for invitation style, paper weight and hue, printing process, typeface, and ink color.

❏ Firm up your guest list and get an accurate count of how many invitations you will need.

❏ Gather information for maps, directions, parking, and other informational enclosures.

❏ Finalize wording for invitation and all other printed matter.

❏ Get an itemized cost breakdown. Order invitations, related enclosures, announcements, and any other stationery needs or wedding favors from the printer. Make sure the printer gives you a chance to proofread a typeset sample before the full order is printed. Establish a firm deadline for delivery or pickup. If the delivery time is considerable, ask to receive envelopes early.

THREE-AND-A-HALF TO FIVE MONTHS IN ADVANCE

❏ Hire a calligrapher, if necessary, and coordinate a time frame for addressing invitations.

THREE-AND-A-HALF TO FIVE MONTHS IN ADVANCE

❏ Carefully check and proofread the printed order. **UPON RECEIPT**

❏ Address outer envelopes and assemble invitations.

EIGHT TO TWELVE WEEKS IN ADVANCE

❏ Buy postage according to the weight of a completely assembled invitation. Mail all the invitations at once.

SIX TO EIGHT WEEKS IN ADVANCE

❏ If you have a standby guest list, use it to mail invitations to replace the first-tier guests who send regrets. Invitations should be sent out no less than four weeks before your wedding date.

FOUR TO SIX WEEKS IN ADVANCE

the invitation to convey. If there is an underlying color, floral, or seasonal theme to your wedding, you may wish to incorporate that theme into your invitations. Generally, the more subtly this is done, the more formal the invitation.

Beyond your personal style and the budget you have to work with, the main elements to consider are the weight, shade, and dimensions of the paper; the printing process; the typeface; and the wording.

FORMAL AND TRADITIONAL

The most formal and traditional invitations are printed on the first page of a double $5^1/_2$" by $7^1/_2$" sheet of heavy paper, usually $5^1/_2$" by $7^1/_2$" inches when folded, or on a smaller single sheet of heavyweight paper. Formal invitations are printed on ivory, soft cream, or white paper. The ornamentation is the ink itself, which is black and typically set in a shaded or antique Roman typeface. Third-person wording is the rule for formal invitations. Engraving, which results in raised print that can be felt on the back of the paper, is the most traditional formal printing style. The shinier, less expensive raised print of thermography is also acceptable.

Traditional Wording for a Formal Wedding
The most common, traditional wording used today for a formal wedding given by the bride's parents reads:

Mr. and Mrs. Henry Stuart Evans
request the honour of your presence
at the marriage of their daughter
Katherine Leigh
to
Mr. Brian Charles Jamison
Saturday, the twelfth of June
nineteen hundred and ninety-nine
at half after four o'clock
Village Lutheran Church
Briarcliff Manor

When Divorced Parents Give the Wedding Together
In the event that relations between the bride's divorced parents (one or both of whom have remarried) are so friendly that they share the wedding expenses and act as co-hosts, both sets of names should appear on the invitation. The bride's mother's name appears first:

Mr. and Mrs. Shelby Goldring
and
Mr. Michael Levy
request the honour of your presence
at the marriage of
Rachel Lynn Levy
Sunday, the ninth of June
nineteen hundred and ninety-nine
at half after five o'clock
Temple Shalom
Englewood, New Jersey

When the Bride and Groom Issue Their Own Invitations
"Miss," "Ms.," or "Mrs." are rarely used before the bride's name. An exception is made when a bride and groom send out their own invitations:

The honour of your presence
is requested
at the marriage of
Miss Julie Darden
to
Mr. David Lawrence
Saturday, the sixth of April
nineteen hundred and ninety-nine
at half after two o'clock
St. Thomas Episcopal Church
Ahoskie, North Carolina

[OR]

Miss Amy Lee
and
Mr. Edward Alexander
request the honour of your presence
at their marriage
Sunday, the first of January
nineteen hundred and ninety-nine
at half after eight o'clock
Montcrief Manor
Sonoma, California

Including the Groom's Family in the Invitation

Increasingly, the groom's family shares in or pays the major part of the wedding expenses. In such a case, it is only fair that their names appear on the invitations. The bride's parents' names are given first, and the wording would be:

Mr. and Mrs. David Sumner
and
Captain and Mrs. Lee Stanley Gonzalez
request the honour of your presence
at the marriage of
Lil Sumner
and
Lee Stanley Gonzalez, junior
Friday, the third of August
nineteen hundred and ninety-nine
at half after three o'clock
Waterside Botanical Gardens
Coral Gables, Florida

Less traditional invitations needn't adhere to the third-person wording style. Nor must they conform to any set dimension. In the case of simple, contemporary weddings, they may be printed on paper with a design or border, often in ink that coordinates with the wedding color scheme.

Although an array of typefaces is acceptable for less formal invitations, simple styles are in the best taste and easiest to read. The type may be engraved, thermographed, or for a very informal effect, inexpensively lithographed or laser printed. A word of caution: Laser printing wedding invitations on the blank invitation forms available at better stationers is inexpensive, but it can also look inexpensive. If you go this route, choose the kind of crisp, formal, easily readable typeface that is favored by professional printers, feed the forms through the printer with great care, take pains to eliminate any remnants of perforations in the forms—and allow time for a major change of heart!

Our joy will be more complete
if you will share in the marriage of our daughter
Carole Renée

to

Mr. Dominick Masullo
on Saturday, the fifth of June
at half after four o'clock
7 Old Elm Avenue
Salem, Massachusetts
We invite you to worship with us,
witness their vows, and join us
for a reception following the ceremony
If you are unable to attend, we ask your
presence in thought and prayer
Mr. and Mrs. Earl Rinde
[or Lorraine and Earl Rinde]

R.S.V.P.

Handwritten invitations on beautiful stationery are most often used for very small weddings and for formal ceremonies when the bride and groom wish to personalize their invitations. Most formally, the name of the recipient is written by hand on an otherwise printed card. This can be done by a calligrapher, by laser printer (provided the invitation is a single sheet and a passable font can be found), or by you or someone close to you who has lovely penmanship.

Dear Aunt Ruth,

Sean and I are to be married at Christ's Church on June tenth at four o'clock. We hope you and Uncle Don will come to the church and afterward to the reception at Greentree Country Club.

With much love from us both,

Laura Jeanne

E-MAIL AND WEB ADDRESSES ON INVITATIONS?

More and more couples are including an e-mail or website address on invitations. Doing so gives guests a fast and convenient way to send R.S.V.P.'s; a website may also contain updates on the wedding schedule. Note: An e-mail or website address is not an appropriate inclusion on a formal or semiformal invitation.

CHOOSING A PRINTER OR STATIONER

Before you settle on a printer or stationer, start with recommendations from family and friends who have been recently married and whose tastes you trust. Spend time perusing the wealth of sample books at local stationers and printers. Catalogs are also readily available from the many mail-order wedding stationery companies that advertise in the pages of bridal magazines; return the postcard provided for this purpose or request a catalog via the company's 800 number. (Note: There may be a nominal charge; plus, it can take several weeks to receive a requested catalog from some mail-order wedding stationers.) In choosing a printer or stationer, consider the following:

Invitations and Other Printed Accessories

- Make sure the company is experienced in designing the type of wedding invitations you want (contemporary or traditional) and can offer informed advice.
- Make sure the company has expertise in the printing process.
- Look for quality workmanship. Request samples to insure that you're comfortable with the quality of work.
- Ask questions: Is the printer/stationer able to accommodate all your printing needs (including, for example, designing or printing such enclosures as maps and directions)? If so, does the printer offer an all-inclusive package deal? Is custom designing an option? If an error is made, how quickly can replacement invitations be printed? Is there any discount for ordering extras, such as enclosures?

INVITATION COST-CUTTERS

- Select standard-size invitations. Those that require oversize or nontraditionally shaped envelopes require more postage.
- Use a local print shop.
- Opt for thermography, which generally looks comparable to, but costs much less than, engraving.
- Choose plain paper rather than something with an embossed or printed design. Pick from the basic typefaces rather than the more expensive ones. Stick with black ink.
- Order all of your printed needs, from invitations to monogrammed note paper for thank-yous, from one source. By doing so, you will often get a better price.
- Limit enclosures. Start by printing your ceremony and reception invitations on one page and eliminating reception cards. Some couples eliminate response cards (and the accompanying envelope and stamp); they include an R.S.V.P. and address on the invitation.
- Dispense with the inner envelope.
- Order extra invitations and envelopes. It is far less costly to print extras with your original order than to place a separate order. Typically, a count of 25 invitations (or envelopes) makes one order, and that should be all the extras you need.
- Get it right the first time, with relentless accuracy checks and careful proofreading.
- Instead of hiring a calligrapher to address the envelopes, ask a friend or relative with wonderful handwriting to do it.
- Plan to produce such extras as place cards, direction cards/maps, and wedding programs yourself on a laser printer or by hand. Or ask a friend to do it for you.

- Make sure the printer or stationer will provide you with an itemized break-down of your costs.
- Make sure the printer provides you ample time to proofread the typeset invitation, envelope, and enclosures prior to printing.

PRINTER OR STATIONER NAME _____

_____

ORDERING INVITATIONS

CHECKLIST OF INVITATION NEEDS

❏ **FINALIZE YOUR GUEST LIST.** Determine the number of invitations you will need to order. You will need one invitation for each couple, each single guest, and if possible, each child 13 or older. Invitations are sent out to whole households only on rare occasions, on the understanding that everyone in the family is coming. (Alternatively, young brothers and sisters may be sent a joint invitation or their names may be written on a line below their parents' names on the inner envelope.)

Create a second-tier guest list, sending out these invitations as regrets are received. Note: This must be executed delicately. If this is your plan, mail the initial batch eight weeks prior to the wedding to allow a bigger window for the second-tier guests. All invitees should have no less than four weeks' notice to respond to an invitation.

❏ **DON'T FORGET THE WEDDING PARTY.** Include invitations for the officiant, the parents of the bride and groom, and the wedding party. Be sure to put their names on your master guest list so that you will include them in any head counts.

❏ **ORDER EXTRAS.** Be sure to order extra invitations (at least a dozen, to save as keepsakes and send to forgotten guests) and extra envelopes (as many as 25 to accommodate mistakes in addressing outer envelopes). You will also want extras to present as souvenirs to your parents.

❏ **ONE ENVELOPE OR TWO?** Formal, third-person invitations are traditionally inserted into two envelopes, an inner envelope and an

BEFORE YOU ORDER: PROOFREADING CHECKLIST

❏ Is the invitation printed on the correct paper? Check the paper stock, the paper shade, the dimensions, and the border or design (if any) against your sample.

❏ Is the proper typeface used? Is the typesetting clean and even? Is the ink color correct?

❏ Is the wording correct? Properly spaced and centered?

❏ Read the invitations out loud. Then check the spelling. Are all names and places properly spelled? Are all titles accurate? Is the date written out, and does it correspond with the calendar?

❏ Do the lines break as they should, with the hosts' names, the bride's name, the word "to," the groom's name, the date, the ceremony site's name, and location, all getting their own lines?

❏ Is punctuation where it belongs?

❏ If the invitation is a formal one, is the wording the formal way you desire ("honour," for example, properly spelled with a "u")?

❏ Is the return address correctly printed on the flap of the outer envelope and on any response envelope?

❏ Check the enclosures. Is the wording correct and properly spaced?

❏ Do all cards and enclosures fit into their respective envelopes?

outer envelope. The outer envelope carries the return address and the recipient's address (calligraphed or handwritten). The inner envelope, which is left unsealed, bears only the names of the people to whom the mailing envelope is addressed. As such, it serves a useful purpose: allowing the bride and groom to be very specific as to whom is invited (Miss Smith and Guest, for example, or Aunt Deirdre and Uncle Stan).

ADDRESSING AND ASSEMBLY

Invitations are always addressed to both members of a married couple. An invitation to an unmarried couple who reside at the same address should be addressed with each name appearing on a separate line. No abbreviations or initials are used except "Mr." and "Mrs." and the postal state abbreviation, if desired. If children are not receiving a separate invitation, their names may be written on a line below their parents' names on the inner envelope. If no inner envelope is used, their names must be written on the outer envelope.

Carefully consider where you want your R.S.V.P.'s sent, as responses and gifts are often sent to the return address on the outer envelope.

ASSEMBLY AND MAILING TIPS

Allow plenty of time to carefully address, assemble, and mail your invitations. Arrange each element that goes into an invitation in a stack, in the order it will be picked up, assembled, and inserted. Ideally, you want to handle each piece only once, if possible.

- Organize the master guest list in useful form, perhaps on file cards or a computer database.
- Before you buy stamps, have a completely assembled invitation (or two variations: one for local guests, another for out-of-town guests) weighed at the post office. Look for pretty stamps that will complement the look of your wedding invitation envelope.
- A folded formal invitation is properly placed into the inner or outer envelope with the fold down and the typeface away from the person inserting it. If the invitation is a single sheet, it should be placed into the inner or outer envelope so that the side with the lettering faces the person inserting it.
- Insertions are placed in front of the invitation inside the inner (if used) or outer envelope. Tissues are optional.
- The inner envelope is left unsealed and placed into the outer envelope so that recipients' names are visible when the outer envelope is opened.
- If you are using response cards, consider marking the back of each card with an identifying number in case guests neglect to write in their names when they R.S.V.P.
- Before sealing the outer envelope, double and triple check that the names on the inner and outer envelopes match up.

ALL ABOUT INSERTIONS

In addition to the invitation, several cards may be printed and sent along with the invitation, as necessary. They include:

- **RESPONSE CARDS.** A conventional twist that replaces the traditional, formal handwritten reply. It provides a space for guests to write their names and to indicate their acceptance or regrets. Accompanied by a printed, stamped envelope.

- RECEPTION CARDS. Included when more people are invited to the reception than to the ceremony or when the reception and the ceremony are held in different locations.
- MAP/DIRECTIONS CARDS. Generally for out-of-town guests only. Written and produced as concisely as possible to minimize bulk. Printed directions, especially when accompanying formal invitations, look the best.
- ADMISSION CARDS. Included only when a wedding is held in a cathedral or church that attracts sightseers.
- PEW CARDS. Engraved with "Pew Number ___" or "Within the Ribbon" to indicate reserved seating for close family and friends. Usually sent after acceptances are received.
- AT HOME CARDS. Used to let friends know the bride and groom's new address. Inserted with the invitation or wedding announcement.
- RAIN CARDS. Notes the alternate location of the ceremony and/or the reception in the event of inclement weather.
- TRAVEL INFORMATION. Help for the out-of-town guests. This can be sent after you receive a response or can be included with the invitation, perhaps laser-printed on a single sheet of stationery. Helpful information may include suggested lodging (ideally a place convenient to the church/reception with which you have booked a block of rooms), the names of airlines that fly into nearby airports, ground transportation services, car rental rates and times of operation—even a list of special attractions in the area.

PRINTED EXTRAS AND OPTIONS

WEDDING ANNOUNCEMENTS

Sent to friends and family who could not be accommodated on the guest list and to acquaintances or business associates who might wish to hear news of the marriage. Not obligatory. Ideally mailed the day after the wedding and may be sent in the name of the bride's parents (traditional) or both sets of parents, as desired. Guests who receive wedding announcements have no obligation to send a gift. For a sample of a wedding announcement, refer to Chapter 20, "After The Big Day."

PERSONAL STATIONERY

Fold-over note cards, usually printed with the initial of the couple's last name (to be used by both the bride and groom) or the bride's name or initials on the front. Often ordered alongside invitations to be used as thank-you notes. Some photographers include a preprinted photo thank-you card in their package, so you may want to consider using that in place of personal stationery.

PLACE CARDS

Used to designate seating at the reception. Should be written or calligraphed uniformly. Place cards produced by computer are acceptable as long as the typeface chosen looks handwritten and any rough edges from perforated forms are carefully removed. Place cards are sometimes decorated with real or drawn flowers or colorful ribbon.

PERSONALIZED FAVORS

Cocktail napkins, matchbooks, and other memorabilia that is printed with the couple's name or monograms—sometimes offered as favors at the wedding reception but completely optional.

INVITATIONS AND OTHER PRINTED ITEMS WORKSHEET

TYPE	QUANTITY	COST
INVITATIONS		
ENVELOPES		
WEDDING ANNOUNCEMENTS		
THANK-YOU NOTES		
RESPONSE CARDS		
OTHER INSERTS		
PERSONAL STATIONERY		
PERSONALIZED FAVORS		
PLACE CARDS		
PROGRAMS		
TOTAL COST		

Invitations and Other Printed Accessories

CHAPTER 7

GIFTS, GIFT REGISTRIES, AND THANK-YOU NOTES

❏ You and your intended should make two lists: one containing any items you want and the other of items you need. Visit stores. If you are starting out with the basics, look at china, silver, and crystal patterns. **SIX TO TWELVE MONTHS AHEAD**

❏ Complete the list of things you want and need. Include the quantity of items in a category (such as place settings). Open registries in the stores of your choice. **FOUR TO SIX MONTHS AHEAD**

❏ Start keeping detailed records of each gift, the sender's name and address, the date you sent a thank you note, and any exchanges. **ONE TO TWO MONTHS AHEAD OR AS SOON AS YOU START RECEIVING GIFTS**

YOUR BRIDAL REGISTRY

The tradition of registering at department and gift stores for china, silver, and crystal is as popular as ever, but more and more couples are also turning to nontraditional registries to select other types of gifts: practical items such as lawnmowers, kitchen fixtures, and landscaping, and leisure items such as patio furniture, kayaks, binoculars, and exercise equipment. Below is just a sampling of the many places where you can register for gifts.

- Garden and home centers
- Department stores and specialty gift stores, both national and local
- Recreational/sports stores
- Travel agencies
- Home entertainment stores

REGISTRIES

Whether you're registering for a formal china pattern or home centered items, *be sure to offer guests a wide variety of price ranges.* Confirm that the store you're registering with will gift-wrap and ship or deliver any items and whether shipped items will be insured.

- Call ahead of time to see whether you need to make a registry appointment with the store registry consultant.
- The store provides a registry form, which includes your name, wedding date, and the address to which gifts are to be sent. Most stores have computerized registries and will give you a computer printout updating the latest purchases. Many national and regional stores also have 800 numbers or online websites that allow guests to order items easily and efficiently.
- A store registry generally keeps all pertinent information on file for up to several months after the wedding date.
- If you crave something from a store without a bridal registry, ask whether the store will set up one for you—keeping a gift purchase log, accepting telephone orders, and insuring shipped gifts.
- Get the word out that you've registered at certain stores the old-fashioned way: word of mouth. Tradition still holds that the practice of including gift registries on wedding invitations is considered tacky and unacceptable. A phone call to you or a close friend or relative will provide guests with all the information they need. Give your mothers and your maid of honor a list of the stores, mail-order catalogs, Internet addresses, and any other places that you are registered to share with guests.
- A national store or catalog service is able to monitor purchases, thus removing items that have been bought for you from your list and preventing duplicate purchases. They will also indicate when items are no longer available. One store, however, will not coordinate with another. Therefore, do not register for the same things at different stores.

REGISTERING THE FAST AND EASY WAY

Registering in national chain stores works nicely for out-of-town guests, who can order easily from the companies' 800 numbers and have the gifts delivered by mail. Online couples can register for gifts on one of the growing number of retail chains' websites—allowing friends and family who live far away to easily place an order at their computer. Start by accessing the Wedding Registries Directory Home Page (www.wedreg.com).

STORE REGISTRY WORKSHEET

Photocopy this page as necessary.

STORE NAME _____

ITEMS TO REGISTER

_____   _____
_____   _____
_____   _____
_____   _____
_____   _____
_____   _____
_____   _____
_____   _____
_____   _____
_____   _____
_____   _____
_____   _____

STORE NAME _____

ITEMS TO REGISTER

_____   _____
_____   _____
_____   _____
_____   _____
_____   _____
_____   _____
_____   _____
_____   _____
_____   _____
_____   _____
_____   _____

*Gifts, Gift
Registries,
and
Thank-You
Notes*

PLACE SETTINGS

How many five-piece place settings you choose to register for depends on your needs. Do you plan to entertain often? Is your extended family a large one? Some couples register for eight to twelve place settings; ideally you will want to start out with four or six complete place settings.

COMPLETE GIFT-RECEIVED RECORD

On your master guest list, record each gift, the date received, the name and address of the donor, and the store the gift came from, if necessary. Included is a column to indicate the date you sent a thank-you note and a column for numbering each gift. You should also create a record of any engagement and shower gifts you receive.

GIFT DELIVERY

Wedding gifts are generally delivered to the bride's home or the home of her parents before the wedding, addressed to the bride, in her name. Wedding gifts may be sent out as soon as the guest receives an invitation, and may be mailed by the donor or sent directly from the store where they were purchased. Sometimes gifts are delivered in person. When gifts are sent after the wedding, they are usually sent to the couple at their new address. They may also be sent to the couple in care of the parents. You may want to make copies of the delivery-information worksheet on page 85 to give to stores.

BROKEN GIFTS

It happens: You open up a beautifully wrapped box only to find what was once a fine piece of china or crystal is now broken into pieces. If the gift has been sent directly from the donor, immediately check to see whether it was insured. If so, notify the person who sent it so that he can collect the insurance and replace it. If it is not insured, you may not want to mention that it arrived broken; otherwise, the person who gave it may feel obligated to replace it. When a broken gift arrives directly from a store, simply take it back without mentioning a thing to the donor. Any reputable store will replace merchandise that arrives damaged.

GIFT DELIVERY BEFORE THE WEDDING:

BRIDE'S (OR COUPLE'S NAME) _____

NAME OF ADDRESSEE C/O _____

DELIVERY ADDRESS _____

_____

_____

_____

TELEPHONE NUMBER _____

ADDITIONAL TELEPHONE NUMBER _____

DATE OF WEDDING _____

GIFT DELIVERY AFTER THE WEDDING:

COUPLE'S NAME _____

DELIVERY ADDRESS _____

_____

_____

_____

TELEPHONE NUMBER _____

ADDITIONAL TELEPHONE NUMBER _____

DATE OF WEDDING _____

DELIVERY START DATE _____

GREAT GIFTS: FROM YOU TO THEM

The two of you can have great fun coming up with unique and personal gifts for the members of your wedding party and special family and friends. Here are some creative suggestions:

- FOR BRIDESMAIDS: lockets containing dried flowers like those in wedding bouquets; antique or foreign Christmas ornaments (especially for a Christmas wedding); half-day spa visit; monogrammed tea towels; astrological chart reading
- FOR USHERS: monogrammed travel bags; antique cufflinks; half-day spa visit; rare books
- FOR PARENTS: silver-framed wedding portrait; basket of gourmet goodies; framed copy of personal wedding vows; flowers-of-the-month club

TIPS ON EXCHANGING GIFTS

You may exchange duplicate presents without telling anyone you have done so. Keep the following tips in mind when considering exchanges.

- If a gift is not a duplicate but something you neither like nor need, you may exchange it, unless it is from a close friend who would be hurt if you did so.
- If the gift is from someone you rarely see, simply write a thank-you note for the gift they sent, even though you've exchanged it for something else.
- You should not exchange gifts chosen for you by your families unless they say you are free to do so.
- When you write a thank-you note for a duplicate gift that you have exchanged, simply thank the giver for the original present. You do not have to say that you exchanged the gift for something else.

GIFTS FROM YOU: CHECKLIST

Not only is your wedding a time of receiving gifts, it is also a time to give them. It is customary for the bride and groom to give each other a gift; they also give their attendants thank-you gifts. But it doesn't stop there. Below is a checklist of people to whom you may decide to give a gift. Your gifts may be given at an attendants' luncheon, if there is one, just after the rehearsal, at the rehearsal dinner, shortly before the wedding, or even after the wedding.

TO:	GIFT
BRIDE/GROOM	
MAID/MATRON OF HONOR	
BEST MAN	
BRIDAL ATTENDANTS	
USHERS/GROOMSMEN	
PARENTS	
YOUR CHILDREN	
PARTY HOSTS	
SPECIAL GUESTS	
OFFICIANT	
OTHER	

WHEN GIFTS SHOULD BE RETURNED

The only time that gifts are returned is when a marriage is either canceled or immediately annulled. When wedding plans are canceled, gifts that have already been received must be returned. If there is simply an indefinite postponement, but the couple does intend to be married, the gifts that have arrived are carefully put away until the ceremony takes place. If, after a period of six weeks to two months, it becomes doubtful that the wedding will proceed at all, the couple must send the gifts back to donors to return.

GIFTS ON THE HOUSE

In addition to registering for linens and tableware, couples can now register for a down payment on a house. Under the Department of Housing and Urban Development's Bridal Registry Initiative, a couple can open an interest-bearing account at any participating bank. Friends and relatives can then deposit gifts of money into the account, which is ultimately used for a down payment or for mortgage payments on a house. A few pointers are worth keeping in mind. For example, donors of gifts will probably advise you if they have made a gift deposit for you, and you will need to thank them for their kindness and generosity, just as you would for any other gift. Questions? Call your bank, or 800–CALIFHA.

TIPS ON THANK-YOU NOTES

Every gift that you receive, whether an expensive vase or a gift of time, must be acknowledged. Thank-you notes take many forms, but all share one common guideline—that they be *prompt*. Ideally, you should write each note within two weeks from the day the gift is received. At the very least, you should have all of your thank-you notes written within three months of the wedding—at the most—especially now that it is expected that the groom shares in this task. Promptness is particularly important when gifts have been sent in the mail or delivered by a store; it lets the sender know his gift has arrived safely.

- A separate, handwritten thank-you note must be sent for each wedding present you receive.
- A note of thanks should also be sent to those who send congratulatory telegrams on the day of the wedding.
- Every thank-you note, no matter how short, should include a reference to thepresent itself. You must express your appreciation for the thought and effort, and never let on in your thank-you note when you are less than pleased with a gift.
- It is inappropriate to send preprinted thank-you cards with no personal message added. If you prefer a card that says "thank you" or has a poem or message on it, choose one that is simple and dignified, and then add your own note, mentioning the gift by name and why you are so happy to have received it.

- No special stationery is required for writing thank-you notes. You can use paper printed or engraved with your maiden-name initials, your married initials, or a monogram of your last name. The paper can be bordered, white or colored, ecru or ivory. In fact, plain, fold-over notes are just fine.

- Some couples like to send preprinted thank-you cards with the couple's wedding portrait inserted into small slits designed specifically for this purpose. These photo cards are attractive mementos of the wedding, especially for those who were unable to attend. Unfortunately, however, the wait for the photos can delay the entire process, taking weeks, even months. Get around this problem by having a portrait taken a month or so before the wedding—whether during sittings for newspaper shots or the formal portraits—so that the cards can be ready and waiting for you when you return from your honeymoon. You can also obtain the cards, minus the photos, immediately, so that you can write notes as gifts arrive. Then, as soon as you receive the photos, you can insert them and mail immediately. Again, always include a personal handwritten message in *any* preprinted card.

 Use the Guest List on page 260 to record all wedding gifts received and dates thank you notes are sent.

WEDDING FAVORS: TO GIVE OR NOT TO GIVE?

Gifts from the bride and groom to their wedding guests, referred to as wedding favors, are necessary only when part of a cultural tradition. Traditional favors include a piece of groom's cake (boxed and wrapped) or a miniature box of chocolates. Favors may also be tiny pots of flowers, miniature bottles of champagne or wine, or keepsakes made by the bride.

The concept of presenting favors to wedding guests has become big business, and many brides and grooms are pressured to feel that they must offer them. While favors are a lovely thought, unless they are part of your tradition, they are completely unnecessary and simply another drain on your budget.

CHAPTER 8

ATTENDANTS

While rules don't dictate the selection of attendants, there are practicalities to consider. The size and formality of your wedding will likely be the main determiners of the size of your wedding party. The average formal or semiformal wedding party includes four to six bridesmaids and as many, or more, ushers. A tried-and-true formula for seating guests expeditiously: Have one usher for every 50 guests. You'll also want to think about who your closest friends are and which members of your families to include.

ATTENDANTS: PLANNING AT A GLANCE

❏ Select attendants, both female and male.
   SOON AFTER YOUR ENGAGEMENT IS ANNOUNCED
   AND WEDDING PLANS ARE UNDERWAY
❏ With your attendants, select outfits.
   SIX TO NINE MONTHS IN ADVANCE
❏ Make arrangements for attendants' lodging, if necessary.
   SIX TO NINE MONTHS IN ADVANCE
❏ Buy attendants' gifts (see Chapter 7, "Gifts, Gift Registries, and Thank-You Notes"). Confirm final fittings.
   Plan attendants' luncheon, if having one.
   ONE TO THREE MONTHS IN ADVANCE
❏ Schedule attendants' wedding-day transportation details and changing locations. TWO WEEKS TO ONE MONTH IN ADVANCE
❏ Mail, e-mail, fax, or call attendants with final wedding itinerary, including rehearsal time and rehearsal dinner information.
   TWO WEEKS TO ONE MONTH IN ADVANCE

SELECTING ATTENDANTS

Generally, the smaller and less formal the wedding and the wedding site, the smaller the wedding party should be. Keep the following tips in mind when selecting your attendants.

- Ask the people you are closest to among friends and family members.
- It is traditional to have at least one usher for every 50 guests.
- Etiquette no longer requires a one-to-one ratio of ushers to bridesmaids.
- Can't decide? It is perfectly acceptable to choose two maids of honor, two best men, male bridesmaids, female ushers, and even to have no attendants at all—as your personal relationships and wishes dictate.
- Before choosing your attendants, check with your officiant about any religious restrictions regarding official witnesses.
- It goes without saying that pregnancy, disability, height, weight, and physical appearance should have no bearing on a person's inclusion or exclusion in the wedding party.
- Remember the financial obligations involved in being an attendant, from travel expenses to clothing. If you have a close friend who can't afford to make those expenditures, you may consider making a private arrangement to foot some or all of the bill.
- Keep in mind that there are other ways of involving and honoring important relatives and friends; they may serve, for example, as a reader at the ceremony, a guest book attendant, or an informal photo coordinator.
- It's good for family unity to include the bride's brothers and the groom's sisters, but it is not mandatory—and usually only possible when the wedding party is large.
- If you are planning a destination wedding, make this clear when you extend the invitation to be in your wedding party.
- It is considerate to ask anyone you want to include as early as possible, preferably shortly after the engagement is announced and you have a firm wedding date, have chosen the location, and have an idea of the size and type of wedding.

KEEPING ATTENDANTS INFORMED

Telephone calls, postcards, newsletters, and e-mail are effective ways to familiarize your attendants with one another while keeping them apprised of your ongoing wedding plans. Details worth sharing include:

- Names, addresses, phone numbers, and e-mail addresses for the wedding party.
- Advance notice of parties and showers to which they are invited.
- Rehearsal and rehearsal dinner arrangements.
- Updates regarding dresses, tuxes, and fittings.
- Information about accommodations.
- Details about their dressing location.
- Notice of any special arrangements made for bridesmaids' hair and makeup.
- Transportation arrangements to the ceremony and reception.

MAID OR MATRON OF HONOR: DUTIES AND RESPONSIBILITIES CHECKLIST

Supporting the bride as a best friend and tireless helper—as well as keeping the bridesmaids organized and on schedule—are the maid or matron of honor's primary responsibilities. If the bride chooses a male friend to be her honor attendant, he is not expected to carry on such traditional roles as helping the bride dress. Some specific duties that may be performed:

- ❏ Helps the bride select bridesmaids' attire.
- ❏ Helps address invitations and place cards.
- ❏ Attends as many prenuptial events as possible.
- ❏ Organizes bridesmaids' gift to the bride; usually gives individual gift to the couple.
- ❏ Makes sure that the bridesmaids, flower girl, and ring bearer are on time for fittings, the rehearsal, the ceremony, and photo sessions.
- ❏ Holds the groom's wedding ring.
- ❏ Helps the bride dress and get ready for the ceremony.
- ❏ Arranges the bride's veil and train before the processional and recessional.
- ❏ Makes sure the bride's gown is "picture perfect" throughout the day.
- ❏ Holds the bride's bouquet during the ceremony.
- ❏ Witnesses the signing of the marriage certificate.
- ❏ Stands on the receiving line.
- ❏ Keeps the bride on schedule.
- ❏ Helps the bride change into her going-away clothes.
- ❏ Takes care of the bride's gown and accessories after the reception.
- ❏ Pays for own wedding attire and transportation to city (not lodging).

MAID/MATRON OF HONOR: VITAL INFORMATION

NAME _____

HEIGHT _____

SIZE _____

DRESS _____

SHOE _____

HAT/HEAD _____

PREFERENCES

DRESS COLOR _____

DRESS STYLE _____

DUTIES ASSIGNED _____

BEST MAN: DUTIES AND RESPONSIBILITIES CHECKLIST

Supporting the groom as a best friend and tireless helper, and keeping the ushers organized and on schedule, are the best man's primary responsibilities. If the groom chooses a female friend as his honor attendant, she is not expected to help him dress. Some specific duties that may be performed:

- ❏ Organizes a pre-wedding party for the groom.
- ❏ Coordinates the ushers' gift to the groom; usually gives individual gift to the couple.
- ❏ Gets the groom dressed and to the ceremony on time.
- ❏ Makes sure the groom's wedding-related expenses are prepared (clergy fee, for example).
- ❏ Checks that the groom has brought the marriage license.
- ❏ Sees that the officiant receives his or her payment.
- ❏ Takes care of and holds the bride's wedding ring.
- ❏ Makes sure all ushers are properly attired and in place on time.
- ❏ Helps welcome guests.
- ❏ Offers first toast to bride and groom at reception.
- ❏ Dances with the bride, maid or matron of honor, mothers, and single female guests.
- ❏ Witnesses the signing of the marriage certificate.
- ❏ Drives the bride and groom to reception if no hired driver.

- ❏ Helps the groom get ready for the honeymoon.
- ❏ Gathers up and takes care of the groom's wedding clothes after he changes.
- ❏ Has a car ready for the bride and groom to leave the reception, or perhaps drives them to their next destination.
- ❏ Coordinates return of rented apparel.
- ❏ Pays for own wedding attire and transportation to the city (not lodging).

BEST MAN: VITAL INFORMATION

NAME _____

HEIGHT _____

SIZE _____

SUIT _____

SHIRT _____

SHOE _____

DUTIES ASSIGNED _____

BRIDESMAIDS: DUTIES AND RESPONSIBILITIES CHECKLIST

It is a misconception that bridesmaids must host a shower for the bride. They are, however, traditionally expected to:

- ❏ Take responsibility for dress fittings.
- ❏ Assist the maid or matron of honor in any way they can.
- ❏ Attend as many prenuptial events as possible.
- ❏ Assist bride with errands.
- ❏ Contribute to bridesmaids' gift to the bride; usually give an individual gift to the couple.
- ❏ Arrive at dressing site promptly.
- ❏ Be prepared to participate in receiving line, if asked.
- ❏ Dance with ushers and single male guests.
- ❏ Help gather guests for the first dance, cake-cutting, and bouquet toss.
- ❏ Look after elderly relatives or friends.
- ❏ Pay for their own wedding attire and transportation to the city (not lodging).

BRIDESMAIDS: VITAL INFORMATION

Photocopy this page as necessary.

BRIDESMAID NAME _____

HEIGHT _____

SIZE _____

DRESS _____

SHOE _____

HAT/HEAD _____

PREFERENCES

DRESS COLOR _____

DRESS STYLE _____

DUTIES ASSIGNED _____

BRIDESMAID NAME _____

HEIGHT _____

SIZE _____

DRESS _____

SHOE _____

HAT/HEAD _____

PREFERENCES

DRESS COLOR _____

DRESS STYLE _____

DUTIES ASSIGNED _____

HEAD USHER: DUTIES AND RESPONSIBILITIES CHECKLIST

To relieve the best man of the double duty of attending to the groom and over-seeing the ushers, a head usher is sometimes appointed. In addition to the duties mentioned in the following "Ushers: Duties and Responsibilities Check-list," the head usher should:

- ❏ Take responsibility for guests who receive special flowers or corsages when they arrive, and guests who are to be seated in specific pews or within the ribbons.
- ❏ Make sure that all the ushers are dressed properly, wearing their bou-tonnieres on the left side, stem down.
- ❏ Instruct ushers in how to properly greet and escort guests.
- ❏ Instruct ushers to ask guests whether they would mind sitting on the other side, if seating in the church becomes imbalanced.
- ❏ Help gather the wedding party for photographs.
- ❏ See that special guests are seated in the proper order, and ensure that guests receive programs when they are seated.
- ❏ Confirm arrangements for transporting the wedding party to and from the ceremony.

HEAD USHER: VITAL INFORMATION

NAME _____

HEIGHT _____

SIZE _____

SUIT _____

SHIRT _____

SHOE _____

DUTIES ASSIGNED _____

USHERS: DUTIES AND
RESPONSIBILITIES CHECKLIST

As the official greeters of all guests at the ceremony, ushers should be in place at least one hour before the ceremony begins. An usher should also:

❏ Participate in a party for the groom.

❏ Contribute to the groomsmen's gift to the groom; usually give an individual gift to the couple.

❏ Review any special seating situations with the head usher before the ceremony begins.

❏ Greet guests as they arrive.

❏ Seat the eldest woman first if a group of guests arrives simultaneously.

❏ Ask guests whether they are to be seated on the bride's side (left, from the back) or the groom's side (right, from the back).

❏ Offer his right arm to female guests (with the guest's escort walking behind) or ask a couple to follow behind as he leads the way to their seat.

❏ Walk to the left side of a male guest.

❏ Hand programs to guests when they are seated (if programs are used).

❏ Put the aisle runner in place after guests are seated, before the processional begins.

❏ Know the order for seating: special guests, grandmothers of the bride and groom, groom's mother, and bride's mother last.

❏ Remove pew ribbons, one row at a time, after the ceremony.

❏ After the ceremony, close windows and check pews for articles left behind or discarded programs.

❏ Be prepared to direct guests to the reception site perhaps having extra maps available).

❏ Dance with bridesmaids and other guests at the reception.

❏ Look after elderly relatives or friends.

❏ Participate in garter ceremony, if there is one, and encourage other single men to participate, too.

❏ Coordinate return of rented apparel with head usher or best man.

❏ Pay for his own wedding attire and transportation to the city (not lodging).

USHERS: VITAL INFORMATION

Photocopy this page as necessary.

USHER NAME _____

HEIGHT _____

SIZE _____

SUIT _____

SHIRT _____

SHOE _____

DUTIES ASSIGNED _____

USHER NAME _____

HEIGHT _____

SIZE _____

SUIT _____

SHIRT _____

SHOE _____

DUTIES ASSIGNED _____

USHER NAME _____

HEIGHT _____

SIZE _____

SUIT _____

SHIRT _____

SHOE _____

DUTIES ASSIGNED _____

FLOWER GIRL: DUTIES CHECKLIST

Often a young relative of the bride, the flower girl is between three and seven years old. She takes part in the rehearsal but usually does not attend any rehearsal dinner; walks directly before the ring bearer in the procession and directly behind him in the recession; may scatter flower petals from a basket or simply carry a basket of flowers or tiny nosegay; and does not stand in the receiving line. Her dress and accessories are traditionally paid for by her family.

FLOWER GIRL: VITAL INFORMATION

NAME _____

PARENTS' NAMES _____

HEIGHT _____

SIZE _____

DRESS _____

SHOE _____

HAT/HEAD _____

DRESS COLOR _____

DRESS STYLE _____

RING BEARER: DUTIES CHECKLIST

This role is taken by a boy between three and seven years old. The ring bearer takes part in the rehearsal but does not attend any rehearsal dinner; carries the actual wedding rings (carefully fastened) or a facsimile of the rings on a white cushion; and immediately precedes the bride in the procession. His attire is traditionally paid for by his family.

RING BEARER: VITAL INFORMATION

NAME _____

PARENTS' NAMES _____

HEIGHT _____

SIZE _____

SUIT OR SHIRT _____

SHOE _____

WORKSHEET:
MISCELLANEOUS HONOR ROLES

In some parts of the country, particularly in the South, it is often the custom to have relatives and friends who have a special relationship with the couple help out at the ceremony or the reception. Those who fill these "honor roles" are often identified by matching corsages in wedding colors and should be included in a wedding photograph with the bride and groom. Their names may also be listed in a newspaper announcement along with those of the wedding party.

Whether you have designated specific honor roles for special friends and relatives or have simply taken advantage of a friend's offer to help out, the following are some duties you can delegate to those who are not attendants.

DUTY	PERSON DELEGATED
Pour coffee or tea	
Serve cake at a house wedding	
Greet guests	
Serve as liturgical assistants, such as readers, lectors, soloists, cantors, deacons, and altar assistants	
Attend the guest book, if used	
Be responsible for the place cards, if used	
Attend the gift table	
Hand out ceremony programs, if used	
Hand out rose petals or jars of bubbles, if used	

CHAPTER 9

WEDDING EVENTS
AND PARTIES

Pre-wedding events and parties are festive occasions held to honor the engaged couple. They can be as simple as a midday kitchen shower or as elaborate as a country-club dinner dance. For the bride and groom, these are fine occasions indeed, letting you bask in the friendship and love of those wishing to share in your happiness.

WEDDING SHOWERS

A wedding shower is a gathering of friends to celebrate a forthcoming marriage with the "showering" of gifts on the guest of honor, the bride, or increasingly, both the bride and groom.

When

A shower may be held on any day of the week that is convenient for the guest of honor, the hostess, and the majority of guests. Wedding showers are often held as a surprise party. Ideally, wedding showers should be held from two weeks to two months prior to the wedding. A shower that takes place too close to the wedding date may be more of an inconvenience than a party for the bride. A shower held too early may occur before the bride knows what she needs and before her wedding plans are firm.

What

A shower may take the form of a morning coffee, a luncheon, a tea, a cocktail party, or a buffet dinner.

Who Hosts

Contrary to some misconceptions, bridesmaids are not required to host a shower, although they certainly may do so. Friends of the bride and groom, friends of parents, and members of the wedding party who are other than immediate family may host a shower, as may an office staff or other colleagues. Tradition says immediate family members of the bride and groom do not host a shower; doing so can appear self-serving—and be seen as a request for gifts. This guideline can be broken under extraordinary circumstances. For example, when a bride-to-be comes from a far distance to visit her future family prior to the wedding, the groom's sisters or mother may correctly give her a shower.

THEME SHOWERS

A shower needs no theme other than to celebrate the upcoming marriage of a couple. Sometimes, however, a hostess narrows or custom-designs the focus of a shower (often after discussions with the bride regarding the wedding couple's needs) to a certain theme. Guests are expected to bring gifts that relate to the theme, and the hostess may even provide theme-related food and decorations. The ideas for some of the themes that might be chosen are limitless. Some are as follows:

- KITCHEN AND BATHROOM SHOWER. Towels, utensils, soaps, everyday glasses, trivets, tablecloths.
- SPA SHOWER. Massage certificates, aromatherapy oils, grooming articles, robes.
- HONEYMOON SHOWER. Travel clock, travel kit, travel book.
- LEISURE TIME SHOWER. Movie tickets, board games, videos and CDs, cocktail glasses and napkins.
- GOURMET COOK SHOWER. Gourmet foods, gourmet utensils, books.
- THE GREAT OUTDOORS SHOWER. Badminton net, flower seeds and gardening tools, picnic basket, Japanese lanterns.
- HAPPY HOLIDAYS SHOWER. Decorations for every holiday of the year.
- ROUND-THE-CLOCK SHOWER. Each guest brings a present appropriate for a different hour of the day. For example, if the hour is four in the afternoon, a guest might bring a teapot and a gourmet tea.
- RECIPE SHOWER. Guests are given recipe cards and asked to make up a menu including their favorite recipes. These cards are collected as they arrive and are put into a recipe box provided by the hostess. At some recipe showers, guests may even prepare one of their recipes.
- LABOR OF LOVE SHOWER. Promises, not gifts, are brought to this shower, where friends pledge to paint, wallpaper, garden, or donate their talents in any number of ways.

SECOND-WEDDING SHOWERS

If the bride has been married before, she may be given a shower the second time around, but it's better to cut back on inviting friends and relatives who were invited to a shower for her first wedding. If the bride is marrying for the first time but her groom has been married before, she certainly may have a shower.

Who Attends

A shower guest list is generally made up of close friends, attendants, and family members. Normally, anyone invited to a shower should be invited to the wedding. One exception would be when coworkers wish to throw an office shower for the bride, even though all are not being invited to the main event. The shower in this case is their way of wishing the couple well.

Attendants and mothers are generally included on lists for wedding showers but are not required to bring gifts to each party. They can, if they wish, bring small, inexpensive but thoughtful presents or pool their resources for a joint gift. The other guests should not be invited to multiple showers, since being invited to many parties puts a serious strain on guests' budgets. In fact, showers for the bride and/or couple should not number more than two, with different guests being invited to each.

WEDDING SHOWERS: VITAL INFORMATION

Use the Guest List on page 260 to record any shower gifts received and when thank-you notes are sent. Record Wedding Shower information in your Address Book on page 254.

HOST _____

THANK-YOU GIFT FOR HOST _____

HOST _____

THANK-YOU GIFT FOR HOST _____

BRIDESMAIDS' LUNCHEON

In some communities, the bridesmaids host a "farewell" luncheon or tea for the bride, either in addition to a shower or instead of a shower. In other regions of the country it is the bride and her mother who host a luncheon or tea for the bridesmaids as a respite in the midst of a busy time—and as a thank-you to the attendants for their presence and support.

When

This luncheon usually takes place close to the wedding, particularly if bridesmaids live in a different community and will be arriving only in time for the wedding celebrations.

What

A bridesmaids' luncheon is little different from any other lunch party. The table may be more elaborately decorated, and the linens are often white or the bride's chosen wedding colors. The bridesmaids' luncheon is an opportune time for the bride to give her bridesmaids their presents.

For the bride and attendants who work during the day, a more convenient get-together may be after work, at a small cocktail party or intimate dinner. Another venue could be a day spa, where they all could share a pre-wedding pampering.

BACHELOR AND BACHELORETTE PARTY

Bachelor parties are not held as often as they used to be—and when they are planned, they are often much more low-key affairs than the traditional bachelor blow-out of yore. One reason is that attendants and friends are often scattered far and wide and may not arrive until the day of the rehearsal. Today, some brides like to have a bachelorette party, similar to a groom's bachelor party.

When

Traditionally, the night before the wedding day or the night before that. Sometimes occurring during the final weeks before the wedding.

What

These days the form of a bachelor or bachelorette party is often a casual "farewell" dinner, usually hosted by attendants and close friends and held in a restaurant or club. Or instead of a dinner gathering, the party might be held on a boat, at the beach, on the golf course, or at a picnic.

Who Hosts

The bachelor party may be hosted by the groom, his father, or his best man and the ushers. The bachelorette party may be hosted by the bride, her mother, or her maid/matron of honor and attendants.

Who Attends

The guest list may include not only attendants and close friends, but also fathers and brothers (bachelor parties) and mothers and sisters (bachelorette party).

APPRECIATION PARTY

Instead of trying to schedule a series of luncheons and bachelor and bachelorette parties, a couple might host an appreciation party instead.

When and Why

The appreciation party is usually held just before the wedding, when everyone has gathered, and is another prime opportunity for the bride and groom to give their attendants gifts of appreciation. An appreciation party can also be held after the couple returns from their honeymoon, if their attendants and special friends live close enough to attend.

What

It's often a casual affair, a barbecue or picnic, especially if the rehearsal dinner is to be formal.

Who Attends

Invited are attendants and anyone else who has given generously of their time and ideas to help make the wedding a success.

_____

_____

_____

_____

_____

_____

_____

_____

_____

_____

_____

_____

_____

_____

_____

_____

_____

_____

_____

_____

_____

_____

_____

Emily Post's
Wedding
Planner

108

PARTIES FOR OUT-OF-TOWN GUESTS

Sometimes friends or relatives will offer to entertain out-of-town guests who are not invited to the rehearsal dinner. This provides those who arrive the night before the wedding with an activity to keep them occupied. It is generally informal—perhaps a barbecue or picnic—and the bride and groom may make an appearance at some point in the evening.

THE REHEARSAL

The rehearsal is one of the most important elements of the wedding process. The entire wedding party is present to learn their roles in the wedding ceremony so that all involved can become familiar and comfortable with the proceedings—no matter how excited and nervous they may become on the big day.

When

The rehearsal is scheduled with the officiant at a time when all attendants will be present. For a Saturday wedding, it is usually held on Friday afternoon or early evening. The closer to the wedding the rehearsal takes place, the better the chances that all will go smoothly on the wedding day.

Who Attends

The following people should be present at the rehearsal:

- The bride and groom
- The attendants
- The bride's parents
- The officiant
- The organist or musician playing the processional and recessional
- Any soloists or readers participating in the ceremony, if possible
- The wedding consultant, if you have one, should also be on hand to help instruct the ushers, line the wedding party up correctly, and help with the spacing and pace of each person as they practice walking up the aisle.
- If there are young children participating in the ceremony, their presence is required only if the rehearsal is not held too late at night. If they attend, they are generally accompanied by their parents.
- Because the groom's parents have no active part in the ceremony, they needn't be present but may be invited by the bride to attend as observers.

What to Wear

People taking part in the rehearsal or attending as observers in a house of worship should dress accordingly. This means no shorts or jeans and, in some houses of worship, no bare arms or legs. When the wedding is taking place at a secular location, clothing might be more informal, unless the rehearsal is to be followed immediately by a rehearsal dinner requiring dressier attire.

What Goes On

The basic procedures covered and practiced at the rehearsal include the following.

- The actual service is not read at the rehearsal. The officiant simply tells the couple the order in which the words of the service come and what their responses will be.
- The couple does not repeat the responses or vows. The officiant might ask the bride and groom to recite one verse, however, so they can find the right tone and volume.
- An aisle runner, if there is one, is discussed with the ushers. The timing and signals of placing the runner is determined so that the officiant knows when the bride's mother has been seated, that the bride has arrived, and when the service should begin.
- The organist plays the processional so that pace and spacing can be practiced.
- Any soloists or readers learn when their participation is to occur.
- The order of the procession is established, and the attendants walk up the aisle two or three times until all goes smoothly.
- Everyone is placed at the chancel to make sure that all can squeeze in and that the lineup looks symmetrical. The maid of honor learns when to take the bride's bouquet and how to monitor whether the bride's gown or train needs rearranging without fussing or attracting attention to herself.
- The best man and the maid of honor learn when to give the rings to the officiant and how to remove the rings if they are affixed to a pillow carried by the ring bearer.
- The officiant should know in advance whether the bride will be wearing a face veil. He can then explain when it should be turned back, and a decision is made on who will do so.
- The ushers are given instruction by the officiant or the wedding consultant on their roles in escorting guests. They should be shown how to offer an arm and how to remove pew ribbons, noting which pews have been set aside for special seating. The ushers will also learn how to help guests exit the site in an orderly fashion at the end of the ceremony.
- The manner in which attendants will leave the chancel—whether in pairs or singly—is also arranged at the rehearsal. All should practice the recessional at least once, just to ensure that they will know how to exit. (The pace of the recessional will be set by the bride and groom on the day of the wedding, and the attendants will follow at a natural walk.)

THE REHEARSAL: VITAL INFORMATION

LOCATION _____

DATE _____

TIME _____

DRESS _____

OFFICIANT _____

OFFICIANT TELEPHONE _____

MUSICIAN _____

MUSICIAN TELEPHONE _____

WEDDING CONSULTANT (IF APPLICABLE) _____

WEDDING CONSULTANT TELEPHONE _____

REHEARSAL PARTY/DINNER

It is customary for the groom's family to host the rehearsal party, but it is not obligatory; if the groom's family does not or cannot give the rehearsal dinner, it may be arranged by the bride's family. If the groom's family is from another town and is unfamiliar with the wedding location, they may elicit the help of the bride or her mother in selecting a location. In this case, preliminary plans are made by telephone or confirmation letter, and the final arrangements are made when the parents arrive for the wedding celebrations.

When

The rehearsal party dinner is held immediately after the rehearsal, generally the night before the wedding day.

What

It may take the form of a formal or semiformal sit-down dinner or buffet, or it can be as informal as a beach party or a picnic.

Level of Formality

The only guideline is that the rehearsal party should not be more formal than the wedding reception will be, particularly if the party is given by the groom's parents.

Who Attends

Those invited to attend a rehearsal party should include the members of the wedding party (except for the flower girl and ring bearer), the officiant, parents and grandparents of the bride and groom, and siblings of the bride and groom if they are not in the wedding party. If the bride and/or groom have stepparents, they are invited with their spouses if they have remarried, but should not be seated next to their former spouses. The wedding party's husbands, wives, fiancées, fiancés, and live-in companions should be invited, but dates are not included. The children of the bride or groom from a previous marriage also attend, unless they are too young. After that, any number of people may attend, including out-of-town guests, close friends, aunts and uncles, and godparents. Junior bridesmaids and junior ushers may attend if the hour is not late, as may the flower girl and ring bearer (if supervised).

The Bride and Groom's Responsibilities

The rehearsal dinner is the perfect occasion for the presentation of the couple's gifts to the bridesmaids and ushers, if they haven't already given them.

Toasts

Toasts should be made during dinner. The host—often the groom's father—should make the first toast, welcoming the guests and expressing his feelings about the forthcoming marriage. He is generally followed with a return toast by the bride's father and then by toasts from attendants and anyone else who wishes to say something. Sometimes the bride and groom stand and speak about each other; they generally end by proposing a toast first to their respective parents and then to all their friends and relatives in attendance.

A SIMULATED TRAIN FOR THE REHEARSAL

If the bride's gown has a long train, she will need a simulated train for the rehearsal. She can create one by pinning a sheet or a length of fabric to her outfit so that she can practice walking with it on. This also gives her maid of honor an opportunity to practice keeping the train in place during the ceremony and the recessional.

REHEARSAL DINNER:
VITAL INFORMATION

Photocopy this page as necessary.

LOCATION _____

DATE _____

TIME _____

DRESS _____

REHEARSAL DINNER GUEST LIST

GUEST _____

R.S.V.P. _____

GUEST _____

R.S.V.P. _____

GUEST _____

R.S.V.P. _____

GUEST _____

R.S.V.P. _____

GUEST _____

R.S.V.P. _____

GUEST _____

R.S.V.P. _____

GUEST _____

R.S.V.P. _____

GUEST _____

R.S.V.P. _____

A BELATED RECEPTION: THE WEDDING PARTY

Couples whose wedding is small and private may decide to throw themselves a party sometime after the wedding to share their happiness with friends.

When
In the weeks following the ceremony.

What
A wedding party can be as formal or as informal as the couple likes and can even have a wedding cake to be cut and served to guests. No gifts are expected—only the good wishes of those present. This party does not parallel the couple's wedding reception so any attendants who live near enough to be there do not wear their wedding clothes. If the wedding party is hosted by the bride or groom's parents, the party is usually in the form of a tea or cocktail buffet. The host and hostess stand at the door with the newlyweds and introduce them to everyone who has not met them.

BELATED RECEPTION GUEST LIST

Photocopy this worksheet as necessary to compile your list.

GUEST _____

ADDRESS _____

_____

TELEPHONE _____

R.S.V.P. _____

GUEST _____

ADDRESS _____

_____

TELEPHONE _____

R.S.V.P. _____

GUEST _____

ADDRESS _____

_____

TELEPHONE _____

R.S.V.P. _____

GUEST _____

ADDRESS _____

_____

TELEPHONE _____

R.S.V.P. _____

GUEST _____

ADDRESS _____

_____

TELEPHONE _____

R.S.V.P. _____

CHAPTER 10

PLANNING THE CEREMONY

CEREMONY: PLANNING AT A GLANCE

The entire wedding day revolves around the ceremony time, date, and place—details that go hand in hand with choosing your officiant. As soon as you've made these basic determinations, arrange to discuss preparations and requirements with your officiant. Include the following in your meeting.

❏ Discuss the ceremony and rehearsal. Determine whether you may include personal elements in your ceremony, such as special vows or readings or the participation of children from previous marriages.

❏ If you wish to have an out-of-town officiant perform your ceremony, consult the local clergy immediately to ascertain related regulations and requirements. Note that you will be responsible for paying the travel, lodging, and meal expenses of the out-of-town clergyman.

❏ Meet with the organist or music director to discuss music for the ceremony. Meet potential soloists. Confirm/reserve the date with all musicians.

❏ Schedule a rehearsal with the officiant, preferably for the day prior to the ceremony at a time convenient for attendants from out of town. Find out how long the rehearsal will take so that you can plan the rehearsal dinner accordingly (if you will be having one).

❏ Schedule religious or personal counseling sessions, as desired or required by your faith.

❏ Inquire about any ceremony site restrictions on music and musicians, photography, videography, flowers, dress, parking, the throwing of rose petals, and other logistical aspects of the ceremony. Similarly, investigate site provisions, such as a room for dressing prior to the service.

(CONTINUED)

❑ Contact your officiant to finalize vows, readings, and other elements vital to the flow of the ceremony. Also reconfirm the rehearsal time with the officiant. ONE MONTH IN ADVANCE

❑ Confirm rehearsal time with the officiant and finalize all details relating to the rehearsal dinner. THREE WEEKS IN ADVANCE

❑ Contact the organist or music director to finalize the music for the ceremony. ONE MONTH IN ADVANCE

❑ If you will be providing programs, begin preparing them or have them printed as soon as all major elements of the ceremony are firm. ONE MONTH IN ADVANCE

CHECKLIST OF QUESTIONS TO ASK THE OFFICIANT

❑ What are the church or synagogue's requirements for marriage? Is premarital counseling required or available? _____

❑ How many guests will the church or synagogue comfortably hold? _____

❑ How long, approximately, will the ceremony run? _____

❑ What latitude is permitted for couples interested in writing all or portions of their ceremony? _____

❑ What restrictions, if any, does the church or synagogue have on photography and videography shot before, during, and after the ceremony? Are lights permitted? Where can the photographer and videographer stand during the ceremony? _____

❑ When can you meet with the organist or music director to select music? Are there any restrictions on the music that can be played before, during, and after the ceremony? _____

❑ Are instrumental or vocal soloists permitted? Can the church or synagogue provide or recommend musicians? _____

❑ What kinds of floral arrangements and decorations are permitted? Will the florist be allowed access to decorate? May flowers be removed from the site after the ceremony? _____

❑ Will the officiant alert you to any other weddings scheduled at the church or synagogue on the same day? If another ceremony is scheduled, at what time? How will this affect your access to the site, the arrival of your ushers, and the use of dressing rooms? May you contact the other bride to coordinate flowers and decorations? _____

❏ Is a room available for dressing prior to the service? _____

❏ Does a wedding in this church or synagogue typically cause enough congestion to warrant or require the hiring of a traffic officer? _____

❏ How early should the ushers arrive? _____

❏ Is there any way to insure that the area in front of the church or synagogue will be left vacant for vehicles transporting the wedding party?

_____

❏ Are there any restrictions on throwing rose petals, rice, or birdseed outside the church or synagogue? Is it permissible for the flower girl to scatter rose petals inside the church or synagogue? _____

_____

❏ Is an aisle carpet or runner provided? _____

❏ For a Christian ceremony: May or must communion be part of the ceremony? _____

_____

❏ For a Jewish ceremony: Who will provide the chuppah and may it be decorated with flowers? _____

❏ Are there any restrictions concerning dress? Bare shoulders or arms? Head coverings? _____

❏ May a receiving line be formed at the ceremony site, if desired? _____

❏ What fees apply for the use of the facility? For the services of the organist, the cantor, additional musicians, the sexton, and the priest, minister, or rabbi? When are the fees expected to be paid? Will the officiant arrange for other service participants such as altar boys or acolytes, and should they also be paid? If so, how much? Which of these service participants will participate in the rehearsal? _____

❏ When are rehearsals usually held and how long do they typically last? Are there any restrictions or attendance guidelines for the rehearsal? Can you reserve a rehearsal time now? _____

_____

❏ Can you offer any advice or suggestions for guest parking? For nearby rehearsal dinner locations? _____

❏ For civil ceremonies: How many witnesses are required? What elements may be added to the service? _____

OFFICIANT NAME _____

_____

ARRANGEMENTS FOR A CEREMONY AT ANOTHER SITE

Even if you plan to marry at a site separate from the officiant's church or synagogue, many of the above questions for the officiant still apply. In addition, you will need to know:

❏ Are there any restrictions on the kind of ceremony you can have if it is not conducted in a house of worship? If so, what? If not, is there perhaps more room to deviate from the standard wedding service? _____

_____

❏ What are the travel needs of the officiant? Would he or she prefer to be brought to the site in a hired car or drive own car? (Note: The couple traditionally pays travel and lodging expenses for a visiting officiant.)

_____

❏ Will you need to provide an altar? A kneeling bench or cushions? An altar cloth? Candles? Any other liturgical items? If the answer is yes to any of these questions, ask for the names of resources who provide them. Ask whether makeshift arrangements will do, such as a table that can be used as an altar or a table runner that doubles as an altar cloth. If the ceremony site is a frequent wedding location, you may find that these items are already available.

_____

_____

A CIVIL CEREMONY

In general, you will need to make few arrangements for a civil ceremony to be held at the office of a justice of the peace or at town hall. The ceremony itself is simple and brief. The only things you'll need to do are fulfill the legal requirements and, often, provide two witnesses.

   If a civil ceremony is to be conducted at another site, such as the bride's home, a garden, or a rented facility, the same arrangements need to be made as those for a religious ceremony outside of a house of worship—the exception being the need for liturgical items that aren't required for a civil ceremony.

   If the bride and groom wish to personalize the order of a civil ceremony, they should arrange to meet with the justice of the peace or whomever will officiate to discuss the length of the service, any requirements, and a list of elements they may add to the service.

MAKING ARRANGEMENTS FOR INTERFAITH CEREMONIES

It is important for a bride and groom of different faiths to make sure that the officiant has no objections to performing the ceremony and that the ceremony site allows interfaith marriages. Take time to meet with officiants from both faiths, especially if you plan to have children; they can advise you on ways to honor your respective faiths in your ceremony as well as in your marriage. In some cases, clergy from two faiths will act as co-officiants. If the dictates of your faiths cannot be interwoven in one ceremony, having two ceremonies, one after the other, is a viable alternative to a civil ceremony. Some special touches for couples of mixed faiths: personalizing vows to pledge respect for each other's faith or heritage or including a unity candle ceremony as part of the wedding to symbolize the distinct religions and traditions that are merging in the marriage.

HIGH-TECH CEREMONY SITES

Some houses of worship have modernized sound-recording equipment and can record your entire ceremony and provide audiocassettes as mementos. Other houses of worship have installed state-of-the-art lighting that makes flash photography and high-beam video lights unnecessary.

MAKING IT PERSONAL: POETRY, MUSIC, SPECIAL VOWS

If you wish to write your own vows or to include hand-picked readings, first check with your officiant. Discuss the following:

*   Determine whether readings must be scriptural or may be excerpts from secular sources. Also find out whether the officiant needs to review your selections.
*   If adding secular passages is permissible, request a copy of the liturgy for the wedding ceremony, and ask the officiant to indicate places in which you may add a reading or a piece of music.
*   Find out whether the prelude, processional, ceremony, and recessional music must be sacred, or if the church allows secular, classical, or popular selections.
*   Discuss opportunities for additional vocal or instrumental solos and your personal musical preferences with the music director or organist.

_____

_____

_____

_____

_____

_____

_____

_____

_____

_____

_____

_____

_____

THROWING ROSE PETALS

If you have your heart set on being showered with rose petals or some other celebratory symbol, be sure to ask your officiant if this processional option is allowed. Many houses of worship don't permit guests to toss things toward the bride and groom as they leave the ceremony for the reception, because clean-up is too costly. If you particularly want rose petals scattered before you during the processional, keep in mind that petals are notoriously slippery. As an alternative to rice or rose petals, some couples provide their guests with tiny bottles of bubbles, used for blowing toward them during the recessional. One warning if you do consider celebrating with bubbles: If the bubbles float onto your gown, they could cause staining. Other options: colored streamers or confetti—as long as they are in keeping with the formality of your wedding. In any case, you should offer to pay extra for clean-up.

Many couples decide to forego scattering anything, for practical reasons. Birdseed is rarely used, since it is hardly an indoor item and many ceremony sites discourage throwing anything outdoors. Rice is almost never used anymore, even though as a symbol of fertility, it is deeply rooted in tradition. Rice can be damaging to birds and other wildlife, who cannot digest uncooked grains of rice. It is also almost impossible to rake, scoop, or pick up from grass and flower beds.

TRADITIONAL ORDER OF THE CEREMONY

1. The ushers arrive at the ceremony site about an hour before the ceremony is scheduled to begin.
2. As guests arrive, the ushers promptly welcome them and escort them to their seats.
3. Prelude music is played.
4. Grandparents and other honored guests are escorted to their seats.
5. The parents of the groom are escorted to their seats.
6. The mother of the bride is ushered to her seat.
7. The aisle runner, if used, is rolled out by the ushers.
8. The processional music begins.
9. The clergy member enters the sanctuary.
10. The groom and best man enter, taking their places at the right side of the head of the aisle. The groom stands closer to the center, with the best man standing on his left slightly behind him. They face the congregation.
11. The ushers lead the procession, walking two by two, the shortest men first and any junior ushers following the adults. The bridesmaids are next, walking in pairs or singly, followed by the maid of honor, then the ring bearer and the flower girl.
12. Processional music selected for the bride's entrance begins.
13. The bride enters, accompanied by her father, both her parents, or another escort, or by herself.
14. The ceremony is conducted.

Planning the Ceremony

15. The recessional music begins.

16. The bride and groom turn and walk up the aisle followed by their attendants. The ushers return and escort the family members from the front pews. The remaining guests exit beginning from the front.

17. After the recessional, the bride, the groom, their mothers, and the maid of honor and bridesmaids enter the limousines or cars waiting for them outside the church. Or instead of entering the cars, they might form a receiving line. If the bride and groom are to be showered by well-wishers, rose petals or bottles of bubbles that had been earlier distributed to the guests are used to "shower" the couple while they exit the ceremony site.

18. If additional photography is to be taken, the wedding party waits to the side as guests exit, then pictures are taken *as quickly as possible.* The guests either wait or proceed to the reception, taking their cue from the parents.

19. The bride and groom sign their papers, witnessed by the maid of honor and best man, at some point before starting the reception.

20. The wedding party departs for the reception (cars should be waiting in front of the ceremony site).

CEREMONY PROGRAMS

Just as meeting with your officiant helps the elements of your ceremony fall into place, a concise program helps your guests follow along. While entirely optional, programs are a nice touch and especially useful for offering translations of segments performed in another language or illuminating ceremony elements that may be unfamiliar to family and friends of other religious or cultural backgrounds. Following is a primer on ceremony programs.

- Programs may be professionally printed or laser-printed, simple folds of quality paper or coordinated to complement the look of the wedding invitations.
- Programs traditionally identify the officiant, parents, members of the wedding party, and friends or family who are serving as soloists or readers.
- Programs often include the names of the processional, service, and recessional music and offer translations, as needed.
- If desired, programs may also provide text for group prayers or readings and include a poem or personal expression of love and gratitude.
- Programs may be distributed by ushers or children as guests enter the ceremony site, or they may be placed in baskets by the door.

CEREMONY COST BREAKDOWN

	COST
OFFICIANT FEE	
CEREMONY SITE USAGE RELIGIOUS	
COUNSELING (FEE OR CONTRIBUTION)	
ORGANIST	
VOCALIST(S)	
OTHER MUSICIAN(S)	
PROGRAM	
FLOWERS AND ANY DECORATIONS	
AISLE RUNNER	
ROSE PETALS OR BUBBLES	
MISCELLANEOUS (AWNINGS, RENTAL CHAIRS, AND ANY OTHER ITEMS)	
TOTAL COST	

CHAPTER 11

WEDDING ATTIRE

For some brides, the selection of a wedding gown is one of the first wedding decisions they make. These days the bride has a multitude of ways to select her wedding attire. She can buy one of the thousands of off-the-rack gowns in bridal shops and department stores around the country and have it quickly altered and fit. She can opt for a custom-made gown—which may have to be ordered at least a year in advance. She can check into fast-growing bridal consignment shops, where beautiful gowns worn only once are offered at unbeatable prices. Or she could put together a nontraditional but still elegant outfit: a cream-colored tea-length evening gown matched with a short veil, or

WEDDING ATTIRE: PLANNING AT A GLANCE

❏ Select wedding gown and accessories.
SIX MONTHS TO ONE YEAR IN ADVANCE

❏ With your attendants, select bridesmaids' outfits—including gown and any accessories—and schedule fittings, if necessary. Have your attendants order outfits, if necessary. Look into any rentals for bridal-party wear. SIX TO NINE MONTHS IN ADVANCE

❏ Schedule fittings; arrange for any formal photography in bridal salon. Finalize accessory selections, including shoes, gloves, and jewelry. Help mothers choose and coordinate their outfits.
FOUR TO SIX MONTHS IN ADVANCE

❏ Attend final fittings. ONE TO TWO MONTHS IN ADVANCE

❏ Make or confirm any appointments with hairdressers or makeup artists. Make sure the groom and his attendants have completed rentals, fittings, and any accessories rentals or purchases. Remind the groom to have his attendants shine shoes before the wedding day.
TWO WEEKS TO ONE MONTH IN ADVANCE

even a simple white suit. The attire for casual brides ranges from frilly skirts paired with lace bodices to a simple dress adorned with a fresh corsage. The bridal gown is but one piece of the bridal party ensemble. The groom has choices to make as well. Other bridal-party attire may include dresses for bridesmaids and the flower girl and outfits for ushers and the ring bearer. Much, of course, depends on the style of wedding: the formality, the setting, the time of day, the season, the theme, the theme colors, and the size of the wedding party.

TIP TO TOE: THE BRIDAL-WEAR PRIMER

Choosing your bridal ensemble may mean learning a whole new vocabulary of terms. Here is a fast primer on the most commonly used bridal-wear fabrics, styles, trains, veils, and headdresses.

FABRICS AND LACE

- SATIN. A favorite choice among brides marrying in fall or winter, but too hot and heavy a material for most brides in warmer months.
- BROCADE, VELVET, AND MOIRÉ. More suitable for autumn and midwinter weddings.
- LACE AND TISSUE TAFFETA. Popular choices in spring.
- CHIFFON, ORGANDY, MARQUISETTE, COTTON, PIQUÉ, AND LINEN. Good light summer fabrics.
- SYNTHETIC MATERIALS. Offer the bride more choices for every season, plus the extra bonus of a gown less likely to wrinkle.

STYLES

Following are some of the more popular and traditional bridal gown styles.

- BALL GOWN. A "Cinderella"-style gown with a big, poufy skirt.
- A-LINE. Just as the name implies, the shape of an "A," slimmer at the bodice and widening from the bodice down.
- EMPIRE. Dress with a high waist that is cropped just below the bust, from which the skirt flares.
- BASQUE. The waist in this instance is several inches below the natural waistline and forms a "U" or a "V" shape.

BALL GOWN

BASQUE ("U" WAISTLINE)

A-LINE

EMPIRE

BASQUE ("V" WAISTLINE)

WEDDING-GOWN DRESSING TIPS

- When putting the gown on over your head, you should always hold a towel in front of your face if your makeup has already been applied. This is not the time for spot removal, and it is all too easy for foundation or lipstick to rub off on the gown.
- If the gown is close-fitting, your hair should be styled after the gown is in place.
- A low stool is a great addition to the dressing room; the bride can sit without wrinkling her dress, her skirts around her over the stool, while she has her hair done and her veil, flowers, or other headpiece put in place.

TRAINS

Trains are either sewn onto the dress or come detachable for ease of movement at the reception. Some of the most popular trains for floor-length dresses are

- **SWEEP TRAIN**. Train draping from the waistline to six inches on the floor.
- **COURT TRAIN**. Train that extends three feet from the waistline.
- **CHAPEL TRAIN**. Train that extends five feet from the waistline.
- **CATHEDRAL TRAIN**. Train that extends three yards from the waistline; more often associated with formal weddings.
- **WATTEAU TRAIN**. Train that drapes from the shoulders.

HAIR AND MAKEUP

The bride should experiment with hairstyles to find the one that is the most flattering and natural and that best complements her headdress, if she is wearing one. Plan a trial appointment with your hairdresser to establish the look you want on your wedding day.

Some brides hire a makeup artist to apply their makeup and that of their attendants on the day of the wedding. If you do, be sure to have a trial run with the makeup artist in the weeks preceding the wedding.

VEILS

Veils come in a variety of lengths and materials. They are often fashioned from lace or tulle, and they may have delicately embroidered edgings and trims.

- **BLUSHER VEIL.** Short veil worn over the face; it often falls below the neckline.
- **FINGERTIP VEIL.** Veil that falls to the tips of the fingers.
- **SWEEP VEIL.** Veil that barely sweeps the ground.
- **CHAPEL VEIL.** Long veil that trails one or two feet from the gown.
- **CATHEDRAL VEIL.** Long veil that trails from one to three yards from the gown.
- **MANTILLA.** A scarf-like veil that drapes over the head and shoulders.

BLUSHER

FINGERTIP

SWEEP

MANTILLA

CATHEDRAL

HEADDRESSES

Bridal headdresses may come either attached to a veil, separate but placed over a veil, or without a veil. They may be as simple as a hat, a bow, or a hair comb.

- **HEADBAND**. Worn around the head.
- **WREATH OF FLOWERS**. Worn snugly on the crown of the head or woven into the hair.
- **TIARA**. Crown rests on top of the head.
- **JULIET CAP**. A small worn by hugging the crown.

HEADBAND WITH WREATH OF FLOWERS

TIARA

SHOES AND GLOVES

- **SHOES**. Satin or sometimes other fabric, such as silk
- **GLOVES**. Kid or cloth

JEWELRY

- Classic and neutral-colored, such as a pearl necklace or a pearl and diamond lavaliere.
- Heirloom jewelry or jewelry with special meaning.

COMFY FANCY FEET

Some brides consider comfort as important as beauty when selecting wedding shoes. Many bridal stores offer beautiful beaded ballet shoes or fancy rhinestone-studded sneakers you can wear in your march up the aisle or simply slip into at the reception for comfort.

TIPS ON SHOPPING
FOR A WEDDING GOWN

Begin looking for a wedding gown as soon as the date is set. If yours is a formal wedding where elaborate, custom-made gowns are often the rule, you may need to order your gown as far as a year in advance. Delivery times can be as short as eight weeks and as long as a year. Consider the following when shopping for your wedding gown:

- Pore over magazines and cut out pictures of looks you like. Clip them into your planner so that when you begin working with a salesperson or wedding consultant, she will know the kind of style you are looking for.
- Consider hiring a seamstress to make your gown. You can find a good one through recommendations by tailors, dry cleaners, or bridal salons. Ask to see samples or photographs of her work.
- Attend bridal fashion shows, usually held in the spring and fall, and visit bridal salons and stores.
- Try on various styles before narrowing down your choices. Don't rely on hanger appeal only. You might be pleasantly surprised when you try on styles you hadn't considered.
- When trying on gowns, wear the same type of lingerie and shoes the same height as those you plan to wear on your wedding day.
- Be realistic about your budget. You won't want to skimp, but surely you can find the perfect gown in your price range. Look carefully.
- Be sure to set the delivery date for a few days before your formal portrait sitting, not the actual wedding day. You can then plan a fitting between the delivery date and the photography date. Your first fitting should be scheduled approximately four to five weeks before the date for your formal portrait.
- Make sure that alterations to your gown are included in the service and price in the contract with a bridal salon. If they are not, ask what the general costs are. Very often, a manufacturer's or designer's gown is ordered by the salon in a size larger than you need so that there is extra fabric when alterations are required. This can be a plus, but if you need few alterations to the size you usually wear, you are paying for charges you aren't expecting. Does the salon charge extra to press your gown after alterations? If so, how much extra? Would it be less expensive for you to take the gown to a reputable and experienced dry cleaner for pressing?
- Before you invest in a gown, crumple the sample gown in your hand for a minute to see if it shows wrinkles.

BRIDAL GOWN PERTINENT INFORMATION

BRIDAL SALON _____

GOWN MANUFACTURER _____

GOWN NAME _____

OTHER _____

MEASUREMENTS

DRESS SIZE _____

HEIGHT _____

WEIGHT _____

BUST _____

WAIST _____

HIPS _____

SLEEVE _____

GOWN SPECIFICS

COLOR _____

FABRIC _____

LACE _____

ADORNMENTS _____

NECKLINE _____

WAIST _____

SLEEVES _____

LENGTH _____

ALTERATIONS _____

FIRST FITTING

DATE _____

TIME _____

LOCATION _____

SECOND FITTING

DATE _____

TIME _____

LOCATION _____

FINAL FITTING

DATE _____

TIME _____

LOCATION _____

DELIVERY/PICKUP

DATE _____

TIME _____

BRIDAL ATTENDANTS: ATTIRE

As the bride, you have an obligation to consider the price of your attendants' gowns carefully, since in most cases they are expected to pay for their dresses and accessories themselves. Consider the following as well.

- Because your attendants come in all shapes and sizes, you should look for gowns that will flatter one and all. Get their input and be flexible. You can have each bridesmaid choose a slightly different style to accentuate the positive for everyone. Some brides, respecting attendants' privacy, won't even bother to ask for sizes or body measurements but let the bridesmaids do their own shopping.
- There is nothing wrong with variations on a theme. Bridesmaids' dresses may be identical in texture and style, but not necessarily in color—and vice versa.
- The number one guideline: Bridesmaids' dresses should match the bride's dress in degree of formality. The material for the bridesmaids' dresses should complement the material of the dress of the bride. In other words, if the bride chooses to wear satin, the attendants' dresses should not be organdy or ruffled lace.
- Consider any religious requirements, such as arms and necks covered, when advising attendants on dress selections. Check with the officiant to see whether your ceremony site has any restrictions.
- The dress of the maid or matron of honor may be different from that of the bridesmaids or her flowers of a different color.
- Make sure all hemlines are the same distance from the floor. Do so by taking your tallest attendant's measurement from the floor up to the hem of the gown and matching the other attendants' lengths to that. If dresses are long, the hemline should be short enough to prevent the attendants' tripping on the church or chancel steps.
- The bride should ask her attendants to buy their shoes well ahead of time, particularly if she is having them dyed the same color. Also, when bridesmaids' dresses are short or tea length, she needs to make sure all are wearing the same color pantyhose.

PRE-WEDDING GOWN CARE

Bringing your bridal gown home means more than just hanging it in a closet. It needs a little extra care to be ready for the big day. Air it out by removing it from the garment bag. Leave in, however, any tissue stuffing in the sleeves or shoulders. Hang in a high point in your house so that the train can be spread on the floor, laid over a white sheet.

THE BEST WOMAN

When the groom's "best man" or an usher is a woman, she may wear a dress in the color family of the bride's attendants, but more often she wears a dress in black or gray or whatever main color the men are wearing. She should not wear a tuxedo, nor should she dress like the ushers. She may have a corsage in the same flowers as the boutonnieres but does not carry a bouquet.

YOUNG ATTENDANTS: ATTIRE

- Flower girls are generally dressed in white ballet-length dresses or in gowns similar to those of the bridesmaids but in a style becoming to a child.
- Flower girls usually wear small wreaths of artificial flowers on their heads or no headdress at all. They may have ribbons or flowers braided into long hair instead.
- Flower girls traditionally carry small bouquets or baskets of flowers, but because the petals can be slippery, flower girls no longer strew them before the bride.
- Very small boys—ring bearers, pages, or train bearers—wear white Eton-style jackets with short pants. When they are a little older, they may wear navy-blue suits instead. If a boy's suit is white, his shoes and socks should also be white; if it is navy, he wears navy socks and black shoes.
- Junior bridesmaids wear dresses exactly like those of the older bridesmaids, although sometimes of a different color. Their flowers may or may not be different from the others.
- Junior ushers dress in the same style of clothing as the other ushers.

SWEAR BY SWATCHES

When you order or buy your gown and your attendants' gowns, have the store or bridal salon provide you with swatches of both. The swatches will prove invaluable, providing a match for shoes that need to be dyed and for bouquets and headdresses that need to be made. Use the swatches when working with the florist to create complementary flower and decorating schemes. Your swatches should be kept in a pocket in your planner at all times.

THE GROOM AND HIS ATTENDANTS: ATTIRE

For the groom and his attendants, the choice of attire is often more cut-and-dried. Following are the traditional choices for formal, semiformal, and informal events.

- FORMAL WEAR. In the evening (after 6 P.M., they wear a black tailcoat and matching trousers, a stiff white shirt, a wing collar, a white tie, and a white waistcoat. For daytime ceremonies, formal day clothes are worn whenever a wedding is scheduled before 6 P.M. The daytime equivalent of the evening tailcoat is a black or Oxford-gray cutaway coat worn with black or gray striped trousers, a pearl gray waistcoat, a stiff white shirt, a stiff fold-down collar, and a four-in-hand black-and-gray tie or a dress ascot tie.

- SEMIFORMAL WEAR. For semiformal evening ceremonies, the groom and groomsmen wear a black or midnight-blue dinner jacket (tuxedo) and matching trousers, a piqué or pleated-front white shirt with an attached collar, a black bow tie, and a black waistcoat or cummerbund. In hot weather, a white dinner jacket and black cummerbund are often used. For semiformal daytime ceremonies, a simple suit-style dark gray or black sack coat is substituted for the cutaway; the shirt is soft, not stiff; and only a four-in-hand tie is worn.

- INFORMAL WEAR. Informal evening and daytime ceremonies call for a simple dark suit. In hot weather, lightweight suits or dark gray are worn. Navy blue jackets can be worn, and accompanied by white trousers and either white dress socks and white dress shoes or black dress socks and black dress shoes. Shirts are soft white with an attached collar, and a regular tie completes the outfit.

THE GROOM AND HIS ATTENDANTS: RENTALS

The groom may send ushers his own outfit's specifications and ask each to rent similar clothing, or for the sake of uniformity, he may find it easier to order all the outfits himself from a rental agency. Shoes can be rented, especially when everyone does not own the same dress shoes. The groom may delegate this task to his best man. The ushers, in any case, pay the rental fee. Formal-wear rental stores generally carry all accessories—such as gloves or cummerbunds—in stock. The groom provides his attendants' boutonnieres.

WEDDING ATTIRE COST-CUTTERS

You don't *have* to buy a brand-new, custom-fit dress for your wedding, a dress you will likely wear once and put into mothballs. Here are some cost-conscious alternatives to buying new:

- GO CONSIGNMENT. Many brides take their wedding gowns to consignment shops, which sell the gown at greatly reduced prices and split the profits with the bride. You can find fantastic bargains in designer gowns, worn once and in perfect shape. Some consignment shops deal with bridal gowns exclusively. Check your Yellow Pages for one near you.

- CHOOSE VINTAGE. Many brides are choosing to wear heirloom wedding dresses, whether that of their mother, their grandmother, or another relative or one bought in a vintage clothing store, where it is often possible to find a beautiful gown at an affordable price. Remember: It's only affordable if it fits and doesn't need a complete refurbishing, because you most likely can't return it—and work on antique clothing can be difficult and costly. Check with a dressmaker or fabric restorer before you buy so that you know what to expect. Ask your dry cleaner to recommend a garment-care shop that works with vintage fabrics. There are amazing processes today that can restore delicate old fabrics to their natural state.

- BORROW. The loan of a wedding dress is a real gift. Pledge to take extraordinarily good care of it and return it freshly cleaned and in perfect condition. If you do borrow a gown, you should show your appreciation with a lovely, personal gift. If the gown is not a perfect fit and requires alterations, your friend must be the one to suggest that they be made. If she does not, you must thank her profusely for her willingness to share, and return the dress to her.

- ORDER DISCOUNTS BY MAIL OR BUY AT BRIDAL OUTLET SHOPS. Many mail-order discount bridal companies and bridal outlets sell designer and popular labels at greatly reduced prices.

- RENT. Many areas now have bridal and evening-wear rental stores, where a bride may rent a dress, just as the groom and ushers rent their costumes. While this can be a practical and satisfactory alternative to buying a one-time-only dress, it is not necessarily an inexpensive alternative. Rentals can be costly; shop around for the best deals.

WEDDING ATTIRE COST BREAKDOWN

	COST	DEPOSIT	BALANCE DUE	DATE
BRIDE				
GOWN				
VEIL				
HEADDRESS				
GLOVES				
SHOES				
JEWELRY				
HOSIERY				
SLIP				
GARTER				
FITTINGS				
HAIR				
MAKEUP				
PERSONAL SHOPPER				
MISCELLANEOUS				
SUBTOTAL				
MAID/ MATRON OF HONOR				
DRESS				
HEADDRESS				
GLOVES				
SHOES				
SLIP				
HOSIERY				
FITTINGS				
HAIR				
MAKEUP				
MISCELLANEOUS				
SUBTOTAL				

(CONTINUED)

	COST	DEPOSIT	BALANCE DUE	DATE
GROOM				
TUXEDO, SUIT, OR JACKET AND PANTS				
SHIRT				
CUMMERBUND				
VEST				
TIE				
SHOES				
SOCKS				
CUFFLINKS				
MISCELLANEOUS				
SUBTOTAL				
BRIDESMAIDS				
DRESS				
HEADDRESS				
GLOVES				
SHOES				
SLIP				
HOSIERY				
FITTINGS				
HAIR				
MAKEUP				
MISCELLANEOUS				
SUBTOTAL				
BEST MAN				
TUXEDO, SUIT, OR JACKET AND PANTS				
SHIRT				
CUMMERBUND				
VEST				
TIE				

	COST	DEPOSIT	BALANCE DUE	DATE
SHOES				
SOCKS				
CUFFLINKS				
MISCELLANEOUS				
SUBTOTAL				
USHERS				
TUXEDO, SUIT, ETC.				
SHIRT				
CUMMERBUND				
VEST				
TIE				
SHOES				
SOCKS				
CUFFLINKS				
MISCELLANEOUS				
SUBTOTAL				
TOTAL				

THE PLUSES OF A PERSONAL SHOPPER

Personal shoppers who often work in or represent a department store or bridal salon, can help in your search for the perfect wedding gown. Some personal shoppers charge their clients a fee, but many earn their fees through the department stores or bridal salons they represent. It is worth investigating a personal shopper, particularly one specializing in weddings. They offer several advantages. One, they know the inventory, what's on the market, and how to find things quickly. A personal shopper can help the busy bride who knows what she wants but hasn't the time to look for it. A personal shopper can also help those brides who don't know where to start or who are intimidated by the whole selection process. Ask at your local department store or bridal salon for a list of personal shoppers.

CHAPTER 12

PLANNING THE RECEPTION

Planning the logistics of a wedding reception may appear daunting at first, but if you have a good idea of the type and style of celebration you want, simply seek out those people who can direct you toward your goal. The expertise of professionals can be of enormous help, whether that of a caterer, reception site manager, or wedding consultant. Let others help you in planning the reception so you can fully enjoy the festivities celebrating your marriage.

THE RECEPTION: PLANNING AT A GLANCE

❑ Select and reserve a reception site that is convenient to the ceremony site and that suits your budget, the size of your guest list, and the style and level of formality you desire for your celebration. LEAD TIME VARIES; OFTEN, A YEAR OR MORE IN ADVANCE

❑ If you are simply renting an empty space and require the services of outside vendors and suppliers, start soliciting vendor recommendations from friends and family. AS SOON AS RECEPTION SITE IS CONFIRMED

❑ Determine with reception site manager whether the site's caterer will be retained, or whether an outside caterer will be hired. IDEALLY, SIX MONTHS TO A YEAR IN ADVANCE, LONGER FOR PEAK PERIODS

❑ Choose your menu and the type of food service. How do you want the food to be served (formal sit-down, a buffet, or food stations)? Work with your caterer on the details of beverage service. IDEALLY, START SIX MONTHS TO A YEAR IN ADVANCE; LONGER FOR PEAK PERIODS

❑ Visit the reception site with the site manager (and wedding consultant, if applicable) to plan the table setup and plot other locations of any cocktail tables, the dance floor, bars, a wedding cake display table, a place card table, a gift table (if any), musicians or DJ, and a receiving line. Check the room's lighting, acoustics, and air circulation. SIX MONTHS TO A YEAR IN ADVANCE

(CONTINUED)

❏ Choose linens and place settings. Coordinate reception decor and floral centerpiece arrangements with your florist, the reception site manager, and your caterer.

SIX MONTHS TO A YEAR IN ADVANCE

❏ Investigate parking options and security (including valet parking, if appropriate), and arrange transportation from the church to the reception for the wedding party and any special guests. Verify directions to the site, and if preprinted directions are not available, have direction cards printed for inclusion with the invitations.

THREE TO SIX MONTHS IN ADVANCE

❏ Provide the caterer, maitre d', reception site manager, wedding consultant, and musicians or DJ each with a timed schedule for all reception events (food service, toast, blessing, first dance, other special dances, wedding cake) and announcements. Clearly delegate responsibility for managing the event's flow so that you needn't worry about it yourself. **START ONE TO THREE MONTHS IN ADVANCE; FINE-TUNE AS NECESSARY**

❏ Make sure any outside vendors coordinate delivery arrangements with the reception site manager as well as one another. **ONE TO THREE MONTHS IN ADVANCE**

❏ Once all R.S.V.P.'s have been received, finalize seating arrangements, double-checking that all guests are accounted for. Submit a final guest count to the caterer or reception site manager, and prepare place cards. **TWO WEEKS IN ADVANCE**

❏ Confirm final plans with your reception site manager, caterer, baker, florist, musicians or DJ, photographer, videographer, and limousine or car service.

ONE TO TWO WEEKS IN ADVANCE

BOOK OF MEMORIES

Because talking time between the newlyweds and their guests is limited, a fun idea is to place a memory book on each table at the reception so that guests can write messages, share memories, and extend lengthier good wishes to the bride and groom than they could offer in the receiving-line crush. Ask a friend to be responsible for collecting the books at the end of the reception.

THE RECEPTION LOCATION: KEY CONSIDERATIONS

The location you choose for the wedding reception will affect the style of wedding you have, the food you serve, and the entertainment you choose. Keep the following in mind when selecting a reception site.

- The formality of a wedding—whether formal, semiformal, or informal—is related to several factors: the location of the ceremony, the reception site, the time of day, the number of attendants, and the size of the guest list. When selecting the reception site, you'll want to see if it's a good fit for the formality that you desire.
- Most sites require a hefty deposit the day you reserve them and have equally steep cancellation fees.
- Look for sufficient rest rooms, a place for coats, and plenty of chairs, even if yours is an afternoon tea or cocktail reception where guests will stand more than they sit.
- Check the acoustics so that your music is neither too low nor too deafening.
- Make sure the space offers good air circulation. A church hall may be a perfect space to decorate, but if it has few windows, it may need extra fans to provide better air circulation.
- Accessibility is important. Think about how your guests will get to the site. If access is difficult, consider hiring mini vans or even a bus to transport guests to and from the reception site. If the parking area is a substantial walk from the reception site, you may want to arrange valet parking.
- Check for access for the disabled. No matter how enchanting, the tower room at the golf club isn't for you if some of your wedding guests are older or have disabilities and the room is up three flights of stairs.

LAG TIME

The lag time between the ceremony and reception is often dependent on several factors—including whether formal photographs of the wedding party will be taken after the ceremony, and if so, the time it will take to do so; the distance from the ceremony site to the reception site; and whether guests will pass through a receiving line at the ceremony site. The ideal lag time is about 30 minutes. While that may not be possible, you should avoid keeping reception guests waiting and aim for as short a lag time as possible.

POPULAR RECEPTION LOCATIONS

There are two basic choices when organizing your reception—full-service facilities or outside suppliers. Hotels, clubs, wedding facilities, and restaurants often offer full-service wedding amenities. Many rental facilities, private homes, and religious fellowship halls generally require the use of outside vendors and suppliers for much of the food and other aspects of the reception. Some of the most popular receptions include:

- HOTEL, CLUB, OR WEDDING FACILITY RECEPTION. Hotels, private clubs, and wedding catering halls can offer complete wedding packages—where everything, from food to beverages to table linens to wedding event planners, is there on-site. Prices are usually based on a per-person cost.
- RESTAURANT RECEPTION. A restaurant reception is a smart idea for the busy couple with little time to plan. All is there in one place: food, service, ambiance, and a built-in clean-up crew. Some wedding parties rent out the entire restaurant for a block of time; others celebrate in the restaurant's private party room.
- TENTED RECEPTION. These days, a tented reception is not simply an outdoor party under a striped awning. Tents run the gamut from simple to palatial, offering everything from dance floors to chandeliers. In general, you need at least one 60-foot-by-60-foot or 40-foot-by-100-foot tent per 200 peo-

QUALITY TIME BETWEEN CEREMONY AND RECEPTION

Sometimes there is no choice in the booked times of a ceremony and a reception, necessitating a long lag time between the two (not recommended but sometimes inevitable). If this happens to you, think of ways to keep guests amused. Out-of-town guests will especially appreciate your planning.

- If you are being married in a large city or at a destination wedding site, hire a sightseeing bus or trolley for a quick tour.
- Plan and plot out a walking tour for those guests who want to see the town or simply go for a sightseeing stroll.
- Arrange for the hotel, motel, or inn where guests are staying to set up a hospitality suite.
- Have a friend hold a post-ceremony, pre-reception gathering to help guests pass the time before the reception begins.

ple for dinner and dancing. You'll need to consider sound system hook-ups, a generator and a back-up generator, ground cover, permits required by local ordinance, and supervisory and other personnel required for tent installation and maintenance.

- OUTDOOR RECEPTION. You're taking a chance if you plan an outdoor reception without a roof or a shelter, whether you've chosen a backyard garden, a mountain glade, or a beach. Consider the season: If you want to marry in the heat of summer, you'll be risking a rain-out from hot-weather thunderstorms or bombardment by pesky insects. If you take a chance on fall or spring, you may find yourself and your guests shivering as an unexpected cold front blows through.

But if your heart is set on marrying outdoors, you can plan wisely and take precautions: Have a backup site prepared just in case. Provide pest-repellent candles and lights. Make yours a hybrid indoor/outdoor reception, with the food and beverages offered indoors or under an awning or tent. Plan your menu around food that keeps well without refrigeration. Choose a menu best prepared in the casual outdoors, such as barbecue on the grill, a clambake, or a lobster roast. Then there are the advantages: being outside enjoying nature, a soft breeze, and glorious sunlight or dancing under the stars or in the romantic light cast by Japanese paper lanterns.

- HOME RECEPTION. A home reception that is largely planned without the aid of professionals is often one where family and friends pitch in and help

UNIQUE RECEPTION LOCATIONS— AT BARGAIN PRICES

Would you prefer a more affordable reception location? Renting the following sites can cost as little as one-tenth—in some regions, even one-twentieth—the cost of a traditional wedding facility or hotel party room. Get helpful advice on unique wedding sites in your area by consulting local wedding coordinators, caterers, and florists.

- Historic homes and sites
- Museums and aquariums
- State or city parks
- Botanical gardens and greenhouses
- Conference retreats
- Town halls
- Libraries
- Vineyards
- Riverboats or barges

with the details, including decorating, parking, seating, and clean-up. By preparing food in advance and freezing it and by keeping the menu and the decorations as simple as possible, a home reception can be both inexpensive and, within reason, easy to manage.

If, however, you are having a home reception with the help of outside professionals, you'll need to give your vendors space to work, especially the catering company.

QUESTIONS TO ASK THE RECEPTION SITE MANAGER

- Is a wedding package offered? _____
- If so, what does it include and what does it cost? _____
- Are substitutions to the package permissible? _____
- What policies and restrictions does the site have for food, beverages, music, flowers, decor? _____
- What are the laws in the state regarding the serving of alcohol? Does the site have a liquor license? _____
- At what time on our wedding day can vendors have access to the site to prepare for the reception? _____
- Will the facility provide printed directions to the site for inclusion in the invitations? _____
- Is there a kitchen for food preparation? Is it fully equipped? _____
- What is the maximum room capacity for guests standing and seated?

  _____
- Are there ample tables and chairs? _____
- Does the facility use and recommend a particular florist? If we prefer to provide our own decorations, how can this be arranged? _____
- What flowers, greens, or decorations will already be in place? _____
- May the reception be extended an extra hour? What would the overtime charges be? _____
- Are taxes included in the costs? _____
- Are gratuities included in the costs? _____
- Is there a room or outdoor space that can be available for group shots to be taken? Is there an additional charge for this room? _____
- Is there a dressing room available for the bridal party? _____
- What are the parking arrangements for guests? Is valet parking available?

- How many people can be on the dance floor at one time? _____
- How large a band or orchestra do you recommend? _____
- Is there adequate wiring and are there sufficient outlets for a sound system, or would the band or DJ have to bring extra cords and plugs? _____
- Who assumes liability if a guest becomes inebriated and has an accident?

  _____
- What kind of privacy will the party have? (Note that at a wedding reception facility, there can be more than one wedding occurring at a time.)

  _____

If the reception site has an in-house catering service:

- What food and drink choices can be offered at the cocktail hour? During the reception? _____
- What is the price difference between brand-name liquors and house brands?

  _____
- What is the price difference between an open bar for the cocktail hour only versus an open bar throughout the reception? _____
- What is the ratio of serving staff to guests? _____
- What does a sample place setting consist of? _____
- Can we sample the food before making selections? _____
- Is there a special rate for providing food and beverages for the musicians, photographers, and videographers? _____
- Is insurance against china and crystal breakage included in the costs? If not, what are additional insurance costs?_____
- What are the choices of table linen colors? Are there choices for china, silver, and crystal?_____
- Can we see a book of on-site wedding cakes and sample a selection? Can we provide our own wedding cake at no extra cost? If not, what is the extra cost? Can arrangements be made for our baker to finish decorating the cake on-site? _____
- At what time do servers go on overtime pay? What would the overtime charges be? Will all gratuities be included in the stated costs? _____
- Are gratuities included in the total bill or are they handled separately?

  _____
- Who will be on-site during the reception to oversee the event? A manager?

  _____

For a unique, possibly outdoor, site:

- Is electrical power available? Is water available? _____

_____

_____

_____

SEATING ARRANGEMENTS

For a seated reception or formal buffet, it is customary for the bride and groom to determine table assignments.

- Request a diagram of your table setup from the reception site manager or caterer to ease the process.
- The bride's and groom's parents are traditionally seated at separate tables with grandparents and close friends of their families. Combining both sets of parents and their obligatory table mates at one table is also fine but can become unwieldy. Divorced parents are seated separately with their respective friends and relatives.
- The wedding party often sits at a long rectangular table, facing their guests, with the bride to the groom's right in the center, the best man on her right, the maid of honor on the groom's left, and the bridesmaids and ushers alternating along the same side of the table. A U-shaped arrangement of tables, in which the bride and groom are seated at the center table, works well for a large group. Attendants' spouses or significant others should be seated here, too, if space allows.
- To comfortably seat members of the wedding party with their significant others, consider using two adjacent large round tables. In this setup, the bride and groom typically sit with the honor attendants (and their partners) and perhaps children from a previous marriage or siblings.
- Don't place the groom's friends and family on one side of the room and the bride's friends and family on the other. Intersperse tables to encourage mixing.
- If place cards are used, don't forget to delegate the task of alphabetizing and delivering the cards to the reception site before the ceremony. Specify exactly how and where the staff should put them out.

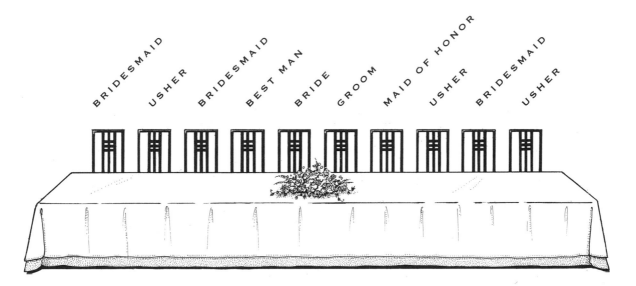

BRIDESMAID USHER BRIDESMAID BEST MAN BRIDE GROOM MAID OF HONOR USHER BRIDESMAID USHER

THE DECOR

If you are using the services of a florist, you will be having discussions concerning reception flowers fairly early in the planning process. Whether you use a florist or not, you should start thinking about the type of decor you will have. Consider the following ways to enhance whatever floral decor you plan for the reception space.

- **DECORATE WITH LIGHTING.** Be sure to check the lighting conditions in effect during the time of day and year that your reception will be held. If the room is too dark, look for ways to brighten it. If it is too bright, inquire about dimmer switches or ask whether some bulbs can be removed. To lend warmth and romance to a reception, decorate with candles and strings of lights: Make liberal use of votive or tapered candles or twinkling Christmas-style strands of light.

- **DECORATE WITH LINENS AND PLATES.** A centerpiece isn't the only defining element of a beautiful table. Take time to coordinate the floral accents of your reception with complementary linens and china. Most caterers or banquet facilities offer linens in a variety of hues, overlays, and textures. You may also have a choice of china. Always ask to see linen fabric samples and actual place settings, and specify your selections in writing.

- **DECORATE WITH FABRIC.** Parachute cloth can look smashing billowing from the ceiling. Tulle netting also makes a sparkling drapery over doorways and windows.

- **DECORATE WITH BEAUTIFUL FOOD PRESENTATION.** Many caterers believe that the food presentation should be decor enough. Indeed, you will need little in the way of decor if it must compete with dramatic ice sculptures filled with frozen flowers, fruits and vegetables cut in wonderful shapes and piled high, or a dazzling color combination of food and linens.
- **DECORATE WITH LITTLE TOUCHES.** In the site's rest rooms, for example, place baskets containing soaps, hand lotion, perfume, aspirin, safety pins, and sanitary supplies, tied up nicely with bows or flowers in the wedding colors. Provide a bowl of breath mints and plenty of tissues. If you can, make sure the lighting is low and flattering. Place a few small vases of freshly cut flowers by the coat-check space. Have the florist fashion something simple and elegant to tack on the wedding facility's front door.

THE RECEPTION SERVICE

Before you think about the types of food and beverages you want to offer, consider the way you want them served. Following are the most common service choices.

SIT-DOWN (OR "SEATED") MEAL

A sit-down meal is a meal at which reception guests are seated and served by a wait staff. Types of sit-down services include:

- **PLATED SERVICE.** Guests are served their meal with the full menu already arranged on their plates.
- **RUSSIAN SERVICE.** Plates are already at the guests' places when they sit down. Courses are served from platters by a wait staff. Often, one waiter serves the vegetables, another the meat, and another the salad.
- **FRENCH SERVICE.** Two waiters do what one waiter does in Russian service, with one holding the platter and the other serving.

BUFFET

At a buffet, guests select what they will eat, either from one long table filled with choices or from several stations strategically situated throughout the room. Guests serve themselves or are served by a staff standing behind the buffet table. There are two types of buffets:

1. Single Buffet Table

This type of buffet is distinguished by a long table, often draped in white and decorated in some fashion. Following are variations on the single buffet.

- If guests are to take their plates to chairs or small tables, stacks of plates, napkins, and cutlery are arranged on the table. If guests are returning to assigned tables, cutlery, napkins, and beverage glasses are already set on the tables.
- Buffet servers may stand behind the buffet tables to assist guests. If there are no servers, guests help themselves.
- Guests pass along the length of the table, going in one direction, and return to their seats or find a place to sit.
- If there are no assigned tables, very often a waiter will carry beverages on a tray and serve guests where they find a seat.
- Whether there are assigned tables or not, if there is staff, guests leave their used plates when they go back for more and take a clean plate from the line.
- At a small house reception without that kind of staff, guests may take their own plates with them when they go back for more.

2. Food Stations

Food stations— a popular variation on buffet service—are often smaller and more compact in size than buffets and often contain one particular kind of food or cuisine. The stations are situated in separate locations in a reception room, allowing guests to move around easily and not have to stand in line at one table. Following are some variations on food stations.

- A chef may be placed at a food station, making crepes to order, for example, or slicing roast beef.

LOOKING AT A CATERER'S PORTFOLIO

When looking over the caterer's portfolio, which is usually an album containing photographs of previous receptions, check for creative touches: fruits and vegetables skillfully cut into beautiful shapes or arranged in eye-catching ways; interesting and complementary color schemes; a variety of dishes; and if you're considering a buffet, well-organized and attractive presentations. The food should be pretty enough to stand on its own.

- Food stations can be theme-oriented or feature a certain type of cuisine. You may, for example, have a Japanese sushi station on one side of the room and a salad bar station on the other.
- Food stations may also be set up for dessert after a sit-down dinner. You might offer a Viennese coffee station, an Italian pastry station, or a make-your-own sundae station.

PASSED-TRAY RECEPTION

Passed-tray service, where waiters circulate through the room with trays of hors d'oeuvres and stop to offer them to guests, is a smart way to serve at a cocktail reception. Sometimes passed-tray service is simply the prelude to a buffet or sit-down meal, or it may be augmented by a buffet table containing crudités, cheese and fruit, or more substantial fare.

RECEPTION FOOD COST-CUTTERS

- HAVE A "PACK-UP RECEPTION." Service takes up a large chunk of any catering bill, with on-site caterers and service staff coming to your location adding as much as 30 to 50 percent to the food costs. If you're having a small reception, you can provide food that has been "packed up" ahead of time for you by a caterer. Most private and supermarket caterers will pack up food to go and give directions on how to heat and serve it. All you do is pick it up, set it out, and provide your own service.
- HAVE A HYBRID RECEPTION. Instead of a costly sit-down dinner, for example, offer cocktail hors d'oeuvres and two or three food stations, featuring crepes, pasta, assorted crudités and dips, cheese, or a carving board. Or have a sit-down first course salad followed by a buffet.
- CHOOSE LESS EXPENSIVE FOODS AND INGREDIENTS. Seafood is more expensive than pasta, for example. You can do this as well if you're having only hors d'oeuvres—simply forego the caviar on toast points for miniature quesadillas, for example.
- AVOID SATURDAY NIGHTS. That's when premium charges apply.
- CHOOSE A "NON-MEAL" TIME OF DAY. If your reception is held at midday or anytime between 4 P.M. and 8 P.M., guests expect to be served a full meal. For a breakfast, brunch, early-afternoon, or even late-evening reception, you can get away with lighter fare, and less of it—a cost-cutting way to serve food. The earlier in the day you hold your reception, the more casual (and less expensive) it can be. Alcohol costs also tend to be lower for daytime events.

OUR RECEPTION FOOD MENU

	NUMBER	TYPE OF SERVICE	TIME OF SERVICE	COST
HORS D'OEUVRES				
MAIN COURSES				
VEGETABLES				
PASTAS/RICE				
SALADS				
BREADS				
DESSERTS				
FOOD STATIONS				

THE WEDDING DRINKS

If you decide to serve alcohol, you'll need to figure how much to serve, the method of service, and how long it will be served. Some receptions offer champagne and wine only; others hold an open bar during the cocktail hour, then serve wine, beer, and champagne during dinner; still others keep the bar open throughout the festivities. Be sure to offer nonalcoholic beverages, including regular and diet sodas (with and without caffeine), iced tea, juices, coffee, tea, and mineral or sparkling water.

OUR RECEPTION BEVERAGE CHOICES

	NUMBER	TYPE OF SERVICE	TIME OF SERVICE	COST
LIQUOR				
WINE				
CHAMPAGNE				
BEER				
BAR SET-UPS				
SOFT DRINKS				
TEA				
COFFEE				
JUICES				
BOTTLED WATER				

WORKING WITH A CATERER

Planning a large reception at any site that provides no food or beverage services of its own can be a lot of work. Entertaining a large group of guests with any degree of pleasure and relaxation may require the aid of professional catering services. It's a choice many couples are glad to have made: Caterers let you be a guest at your own party. Consider the following when shopping for a caterer.

- **DO YOU NEED A CATERER?** The rule of thumb: Hiring a caterer is recommended for a reception of more than 30 guests.
- **A CATERER'S SERVICES**. Depending on the size of the catering company, a caterer can provide the food alone or the works: food, beverages, the wedding cake, the serving staff, crystal and china, tables, chairs, and linens. Some even provide tents, dance floors, and party decorations—or can lead you to reliable suppliers and vendors. A caterer's experience can be extremely valuable in deciding how well-equipped the site is, where to place tables, how many guests can be accommodated comfortably, how many staff will be required, and any number of other details essential to the perfect reception.
- **FINDING A CATERER**. The best way to find a reliable caterer is to ask friends for recommendations. Never, ever, use a caterer without checking his references. And it's always wise to sample the caterer's food.
- **USING AN ON-SITE CATERER**. The on-site caterer at your reception location can be a convenient and cost-efficient alternative to renting a space and hiring independent vendors.
- **CATERING CHARGES**. Caterers generally set prices based on a per-person figure, a figure that varies from region to region, state to state, and urban area to rural area. Costs are dependent on other factors as well: the formality of the occasion, the time of day, the day of the week, the number of guests, what kind of food service you choose, how you choose to serve alcohol and other beverages, and the number of service people needed for the job. Make sure to have the caterer give you an itemized cost breakdown—everything down to the last canapé should be specified in the contract.
- **GETTING STARTED**. If you have your sights set on an off-site caterer, set up a preliminary meeting with the caterer at his office. If all goes well, set up a food tasting. Ask for a variety of dishes, from hors d'oeuvres to a main course to a dessert.

ALCOHOLIC BEVERAGE COST-CUTTERS

Cost-reducing drink and service options include these:

- HAVE A SOFT BAR INSTEAD OF A FULL BAR. At a soft bar, guests may order champagne; beer; nonalcoholic beer; red and white wine; regular and diet sodas (with and without caffeine); iced tea; juices; and coffee, tea, and mineral water. It is a good idea, however, to know your guests' tastes before going with this choice. If your guests are used to cocktails, it might be wise to have a full bar and fewer guests instead.

- OFFER A WHITE BAR. The regular nonalcoholic beverages are served, along with only "white" alcoholic beverages: vodka, gin, champagne, and white wine. Plan according to your guests' preferences; a full bar and fewer guests might be the best solution.

- BUY YOUR OWN LIQUOR. Some caterers will let you buy your own liquor, whether your reception is at home or at a catering facility. Or they will buy it for you and bill you at cost, plus a small percentage for labor. Often this comes in the form of a cork fee— a per-bottle fee charged by the caterer to open and serve liquor you bring in. Keep in mind that whatever you buy, you bear the responsibility of pickup and delivery. Plus, most liquor stores will refund your money if you return unopened liquor bottles. The unopened bottles of liquor will have to be packed and transported from the reception site. To figure out how much you'll need to buy, consider the following formula.

For every 10 guests have:

3 fifths each of vodka, scotch, and bourbon—or the liquors favored by your guests
5 bottles of wine
5 six-packs of beer

- CHOOSE LESS-EXPENSIVE HOUSE BRANDS. If you decide to serve liquor but want to save money, choose house brands rather than premium, name-brand liquors.

- GLASS INSTEAD OF PLASTIC. If yours is an outdoor wedding where alcohol is served, it costs roughly the same and may even be cheaper to rent real (and sturdier) glasses than to buy plastic. Plus, it's more elegant.

- CHOOSE A CONSUMPTION BAR. If your guests are light drinkers, paying the per-drink fee of a consumption bar may cost less than paying the flat liquor fee of an open bar, which is based on a per-person, per-hour rate. Find out what the per-person charge covers before deciding. If it is based on an average of five or six drinks per person for the duration of the reception, and you are also serving wine with dinner and champagne for toasting, you might decide on the per-drink rate instead—it is unlikely that each guest will consume that many glasses of liquor along with the wine.

CHECKLIST OF QUESTIONS TO ASK
WHEN SELECTING A CATERER

- ❏ What size and style of weddings do you typically cater? _____
- ❏ What types of wedding packages are available, and what do they cost?

  _____

- ❏ Are substitutions permissible? _____
- ❏ What food and drink choices can be offered during the cocktail hour? How will they be served? What food and drink selections can be served during the reception? Can we sample selections before making choices?

  _____

- ❏ What styles of service (sit-down, buffet, food stations) are available, and what are the comparative costs? _____
- ❏ What is the price differential for serving brand-name liquors versus house brands? Is a champagne toast included? Is a choice of wine with dinner included? What wine and beer choices will be offered? Can you supply your own liquor? _____
- ❏ What is the cost to have an open bar only for the cocktail hour? To have an open bar for the entire reception? _____
- ❏ What is the exact ratio of serving staff to guests? _____
- ❏ What does a sample place setting consist of? _____
- ❏ Is insurance against china and crystal breakage included in the costs? If not, what additional charges apply? _____
- ❏ How many guests can be comfortably seated at each table? (Check a table set for this number to make sure you agree.) How many tables will be needed and how can they be arranged? _____
- ❏ What are the choices of table linens (color and style), chairs (color and style), and cocktail and dining tables (shapes and sizes)? Are there choices for china, silver, and crystal? _____
- ❏ Is a wedding cake included in the package price? Can we review a sample book and taste a selection of cakes? Is it possible to bring in a cake from an outside bakery at no extra cost? If not, what fees apply? Can arrangements be made for our baker to finish decorating the cake on the premises?
- ❏ What delivery charges apply? _____
- ❏ Will all gratuities and taxes be included in the stated costs? If not, what are the standard tip and tax amounts? _____

  _____

HOW MUCH CHAMPAGNE?

As a general rule you'll need one case of champagne—roughly 100 glasses of bubbly—for every 20 to 25 guests.

- ❏ May tents, marquees, portable toilets, or a dance floor be rented? What are the costs? _____
- ❏ What special rate and accommodations can be made for providing food and beverages to musicians, photographers, and videographers?
  _____
- ❏ What special rate and accommodations can be made for providing food and beverages to children? _____
- ❏ Are there additional fees for the rental of linens, china, flatware, crystal, tables, and chairs? Are there additional fees for setup and cleanup?
  _____
- ❏ Are coat check and valet parking personnel provided? _____
- ❏ Is there any surcharge for heat or air-conditioning? _____
- ❏ Are flowers, decorations, or garnishes provided? _____
- ❏ What is the payment schedule and in what form (check, credit card, certified check) must the final balance be paid? _____
  _____
- ❏ When and in what form must the final guest count be provided? _____
  _____
- ❏ What is the charge if the reception should run overtime? _____

 CATERER NAME _____
_____

PLANNING TRANSPORTATION

Consider the following when planning the type of transportation you'll need for transporting the wedding party from one site to the next.

- If you plan to hire limousines, begin looking for a reputable company the minute your ceremony and reception sites are confirmed. The sooner, the better: Rented limos are in high demand at peak times.
- Consider the number of cars you need. You should have:
  - One for the bride and her father to the ceremony and for the bride and groom to the reception.
  - A second car for the bride's mother, any children in the wedding party, and any attendants who will ride with the bride's mother and father to the reception.
  - A third car for the rest of the bride's attendants.
  - If the sky's the limit and you want to hire additional cars for special guests, grandmothers, or whomever, count them in.
- Don't try to cram the entire wedding party in with you on the way to the reception.
- Even if the car is a huge stretch limo, enjoy the luxury and the romance of having your mate alone with you, if only for a few minutes. This will very likely be the first time you have been alone all day and most probably the last time you will be alone until you leave the reception. Savor the moment.
- Drive the route to get the timing down so that you can give any hired car service an estimate of the hours you will need them. Allow time for traffic tie-ups.

PACK A FOOD BASKET

Have your caterer pack a basket of food for the two of you to take home after the reception, whether you're on the road to your honeymoon or relaxing in a hotel room. Often the bride and groom aren't able to partake of the food at their own reception, at least not in a leisurely manner. See about adding a bottle of champagne, two champagne flutes, some napkins and utensils, and two pieces of wedding cake.

CHECKLIST OF QUESTIONS TO ASK CAR/LIMOUSINE SERVICE

- ❏ How many and what size cars will I need to transport (however many) people? _____
- ❏ What kinds of cars do you have? _____
- ❏ May I select the ones I want to use? _____
- ❏ Do you have a minimum number of hours for a contract? _____
- ❏ How are your rates structured? _____
- ❏ Are any services included in your rates? _____
- ❏ Are gratuities included in the bill? _____
- ❏ What deposit is required? Is there a cancellation clause available? _____
- ❏ What is the preferred method of payment? _____
- ❏ How will the drivers be attired? _____

CAR/LIMOUSINE SERVICE _____

TIME OF SERVICE _____

PICK-UP LOCATION _____

NUMBER OF PEOPLE TO BE TRANSPORTED _____

NUMBER OF VEHICLES _____

EXACT VEHICLES TO BE USED, INCLUDING VEHICLE IDENTIFICATION

NUMBERS OF THE ONES YOU HAVE SELECTED _____

LIABILITY COVERAGE FOR THE COMPANY AS WELL AS FOR YOU, FOR

ACCIDENTS AND DAMAGES _____

RATE FOR EACH VEHICLE, WITH NUMBER OF HOURS INDICATED _____

ADDITIONAL FEES, SUCH AS TAXES AND GRATUITIES _____

DEPOSIT _____

CANCELLATION INFORMATION _____

DATE WHEN BALANCE IS DUE _____

PAYMENT METHOD _____

FINAL DROP-OFF POINT FOR EACH CAR _____

HOW THE BAR IS TO BE STOCKED _____

OTHER AMENITIES _____

PARKING SECURITY

You may require some form of parking security for your guests' cars. Consider the following when checking into parking security.

- Generally, hotels provide valet parking and security. Clubs, wedding halls, and rental facilities usually do not. Call to confirm.
- If your reception is held at a private residence, call the police to find out about local ordinances so that guests' cars won't get ticketed or towed. If the area already has considerable traffic congestion, you will probably need an off-duty police officer or a security guard as well as valet parking attendants.
- When hiring parking security professionals, check that the company is fully insured and licensed, and ask that attendants be neatly dressed and courteous.

RECEPTION COST BREAKDOWN

	COST	DEPOSIT	BALANCE DUE	DATE
LOCATION RENTAL				
CATERER: FOOD				
CATERER: BEVERAGES				
WEDDING CAKE				
WAITERS AND BARTENDERS				
LINENS, PLACE SETTINGS, AND CRYSTAL				
RENTAL OF TABLES AND CHAIRS				
OTHER EQUIPMENT RENTALS (TENT, PORTABLE TOILETS, DANCE FLOOR, ETC.)				
FLOWERS				
OTHER DECORATIONS				
MUSICIANS/DJ				
LIMOUSINES/TRANSPORTATION				
PARKING ATTENDANT				
COAT CHECK				
GRATUITIES				
TOTAL				

CHAPTER 13

FLOWERS

lowers at weddings are used in nearly every aspect of the celebration, from the decoration of church pews to topping the wedding cake. Many couples consider flowers to be the key design element in their wedding celebrations and have them everywhere: in the hands of attendants; given to parents, stepparents, and grandparents; in centerpieces, on mantels, draped around candles, adorning buffet tables, and guarding main entranceways—even garnishing serving platters. The abundance of colorful, fragrant, showy flowers underscores the festive nature of the occasion. Flowers make a joyous statement, celebrating the full blossoming of romantic love.

FLOWERS:
PLANNING AT-A-GLANCE

❑ Begin researching floral selections.
   AS SOON AS YOU BECOME ENGAGED

❑ Set up florist appointments and develop your Wedding Flowers Itemized Wish List (on page 174) as a guide.
   EIGHT TO TWELVE MONTHS IN ADVANCE

❑ Finalize floral plans and ask the florist for an itemized cost breakdown. Set up a delivery schedule and confirm with the site manager. If you are decorating on your own with flowers from a florist or nursery, get a cost breakdown and set up a delivery schedule.
   SIX TO TWELVE MONTHS IN ADVANCE

❑ Make arrangements to rent or borrow large plants or ferns.
   TWO WEEKS TO ONE MONTH IN ADVANCE

❑ Call the florist for a final check and to reconfirm dates and delivery times and addresses.
   ONE TO TWO WEEKS IN ADVANCE

LOCATION, LOCATION

Before you begin formalizing your floral plans, discuss with your contacts at both the locations (ceremony and reception) whether the site includes restrictions and how to ensure access for decorating. Getting clearance to install your floral decorations is imperative. It would be a tremendous disappointment, not to mention a colossal waste of time and effort, to finalize your floral plans and then learn that the florists weren't allowed at the site.

CHECKLIST OF QUESTIONS TO ASK LOCATION MANAGERS

Before you sign any contracts binding you to a location, find out whether the site comes with any restrictions. Below are some sample questions to ask the location manager or contact at the ceremony and reception sites:

CEREMONY LOCATION

❏ Are there any decorating restrictions or rules? _____
_____

❏ At what time may decorations be delivered and how will access be arranged? _____
_____

❏ What is the name of the usual florist for church or synagogue weekly flowers? _____
_____

❏ Are any other weddings or ceremonies planned on the same day as your wedding? _____

❏ Are candles permitted as decorations other than within the sanctuary? Do local fire codes prohibit them? _____

❏ If you want to use an aisle runner, does the ceremony site provide one, or do you need to order one from the florist? _____

❏ Get the site contact name and number and write it down in your planner. Provide the name and number to your florist. _____
_____

❏ Are centerpieces and other decorations included in the contract, or do you have to provide your own flowers and decorations? If the former, may you exclude it from the contract and use your own florist? What percentage of the contract do flowers represent? _____

❏ What, if any, decorations will already be in place? _____

❏ Are there any decorating restrictions or rules? _____

❏ At what time may decorations be delivered and what access will the florist be given to put them in place? _____

❏ May flowers be taken by guests after the reception? Since you are paying for them, the answer should be yes, unless you are using the facility's own containers or have other plans for the flowers. _____

PRE-PLANNING: GATHERING IDEAS

You will want to put a good deal of thought into your floral designs, especially if you plan to use a lot of flowers and want your wedding celebrations to have a well-integrated theme and color scheme. You may find inspiration from bridal magazines, interior design and home magazines, floral websites, flower shows, and photography and garden books. Visit nurseries and well-known gardens and talk to newlyweds who have been through the process. Your flower selections may be based on symbolic meaning or chosen for seasonal freshness, mix-and-match qualities, color, size, fragrance, or simply aesthetic pleasure. Following are some fun and interesting ways to select your flowers.

ALLERGIC TO FLOWERS?

If flowers make you sneeze, you can carry a beautiful arrangement of silk flowers, a Victorian-era fan with satin rosettes and ribbons, or a prayer book topped with a single white silk orchid (symbolizing rare beauty), or a rose (for love).

Flowers

SELECTING FLOWERS BY SEASON

Buying flowers in season often means getting the loveliest and most fragrant blossoms available. Although the advances of modern technology have resulted in the year-round availability of formerly hard-to-get flowers, you can still cut costs by using seasonal flowers that are in bloom locally. They don't need to be shipped, they can be cut close to the time they will be used, and they tend to be hardier than those that are forced in a greenhouse, out of season. Following is a list of seasonal flowers.

SPRINGTIME FLOWERS

apple blossom
cherry blossom
daffodil
dogwood
forsythia
iris
jonquil
larkspur
lilac
lily
lily of the valley
peony
sweet pea
tulip
violet

SUMMERTIME FLOWERS

aster
calla lily
dahlia
daisy
geranium
hydrangea
larkspur
roses
stock

FALL FLOWERS

aster
chrysanthemum
dahlia
marigold
Shasta daisy
zinnia

YEAR-ROUND FLOWERS

Readily available year-round flowers are ones that are grown in greenhouses but that are not rare or difficult to grow.

baby's breath
bachelor button
carnation
delphinium
gardenia
ivy
lily
orchid
rose
stephanotis

SELECTING FLOWERS BY COLOR

Many couples plan their wedding's floral color scheme around favorite colors—and often those favorite colors center around the bridal attendants' dresses, since the bridal dress is likely to be some variation of white. The color of the attendants' outfits, in turn, may be determined by the season. Below are some flower suggestions for bouquets, headdresses, and all-around decor that will complement the colors of your wedding party.

SPRING/SUMMER

LILAC	*violets • larkspur • lilacs • calla lilies*
PINK	*roses • peonies • camellias • gardenias*
YELLOW	*daisies • dahlias • red tulips • narcissus • freesia*
MINT GREEN	*daisies • jonquils • forsythia • ivy*

ROSES, TULIPS,   NARCISSUS   ROSES   GARDENIA   FREESIA
DAISIES

FALL/WINTER

MIDNIGHT BLUE OR NAVY	*blue delphinium • orchids • bachelor buttons*
AUBERGINE	*gladiola • iris • violet • baby's breath*
BURGUNDY	*red roses • carnations • asters*
HUNTER GREEN	*roses • poinsettia • poppies*
GOLD	*marigolds • chrysanthemums • zinnias*
SILVER	*calla lilies • Cattleya orchids • orange blossoms • white roses*

IRISES, ROSES,   CATTLEYA   STEPHANOTIS   MINI   CALLA
CARNATIONS   ORCHIDS   CARNATIONS   LILIES

SELECTING FLOWERS BY HARDINESS

The hardiest flowers stay fresh and don't wilt after a long day of celebrating. The following are some of the flower kingdom's most long-lasting blooms.

baby's breath	ivy
bachelor button	lily
carnation	orchid
daisy	rose
delphinium	stephanotis
gardenia	

SELECTING FLOWERS FOR THE FRAGRANCE

A popular trend is including fragrance in your overall wedding theme, using flowers, herbs, and greenery not just for their visual appeal but for their perfume.

bay laurel	lily of the valley
carnation	magnolia blossom
freesia	mint
gardenia	narcissus
hyacinth	rose (old-fashioned or tea)
jasmine	stephanotis
lavender	violet
lilac	wisteria

DRYING YOUR OWN BOUQUET

If you want to save your bouquet, talk to your florist about using flowers that dry well, such as roses and baby's breath. Hang your bouquet upside down in a dry, dark place before you depart for your honeymoon and leave it for two weeks. Display it carefully—dried flowers are especially fragile.

FLORAL COST-CUTTERS

If you're working within a tight budget, there are many clever ways to save money while planning your wedding decor.

- Cut and arrange your own flowers, then have friends and family help decorate the ceremony and reception sites on the day of the wedding.
- Combine your own flowers with those ordered and arranged by a florist. For example, you could have the florist make centerpieces for the reception, then place fresh-cut cherry blossom branches from your aunt's orchard in vases at the entrance. Or you and your bridesmaids could carry a loose bunch of flowers you pick yourself and tie with a woody stem. Have the florist create nosegays made for the flower girl and special guests.
- Provide your own backyard blooms but give the florist the responsibility of cutting, arranging, and decorating them. That way, you'll enjoy your favorite flowers—and save money in the process—but won't have to do all the work.
- Make your own bouquets, corsages, and boutonnieres ahead of time and refrigerate them.
- Rent decorations. It is often more cost efficient to rent rather than buy potted plants, large palms or ferns, topiaries, and flowers for your ceremony and/or reception sites. Local nurseries often rent big potted plants.
- Use the ceremony flowers at your reception. Delegate the task of transporting the flowers to a friend or hire a service to whisk them away from the ceremony after guests exit and deliver them promptly to the reception site, where there is someone ready to place them correctly and add water if the arrangements have been emptied out during transport.
- Combine fresh flowers with silk or dried. Silk is a good choice for two reasons: It is about one-third the cost of fresh—and it lasts forever. Dried flowers can be prepared in advance from your own garden's bounty.
- Have attendants carry a single flower, such as a long-stemmed rose trailing a ribbon.
- Make fruit and vegetable centerpieces; use purple eggplant, red, yellow, and green peppers, squash, artichokes, pomegranates, apples, and grapes. Intertwine with vines of fresh-cut nasturtiums.
- Use garlands of fresh greenery, tied with colorful ribbons, in place of flower garlands.
- Use inexpensive filler such as sprays of greenery or baby's breath to plump up your flower arrangements.

THE WEDDING FLOWERS
ITEMIZED WISH LIST

How Many?

Whether you've chosen a florist or not, you'll need to come up with a thorough list of needs and top priorities. What is the most important floral expenditure? Can you splurge on this and rely on simple choices for the less important arrangements?

The bride and her attendants traditionally carry bouquets, from formal white bouquets to informal colorful, loose, and cascading bouquets. A boutonniere, generally a small, understated flower wired with greens, is traditionally worn by the groom and his attendants. The parents of the bride and the groom are often given flowers to wear, either as boutonnieres, corsages, or small bouquets. Yet the range of floral decorations can go far beyond bridal party bouquets and altar decorations. You may want a plant for each entranceway, flowers to garnish serving platters, flower sprays for candles, bouquets for wedding helpers and grandparents—even a beribboned flower twined around the cake knife. Use the following list as a guide to plan your floral design, whether you are collaborating with a florist or floral designer or planning to do the arrangements yourself.

First, fill out "The Basics" information list on the next page, which will guide you and your florist throughout the planning.

FREEZE-DRIED FLOWERS

Many florists now have the technical capacity to freeze-dry flowers—preserving them for all time in much the same state they were when fresh. You can preserve your bridal bouquet and keep it on display with the freeze-drying method. After the wedding, bridal bouquets are taken apart and each component freeze-dried separately. The arrangement is then put back together and the bouquet is placed in a glass box, frozen in time and on display for your children—and even your grandchildren—to see.

THE BASICS

WEDDING DATE _____

CEREMONY LOCATION _____

TIME _____

DESCRIPTION _____

NUMBER OF PEWS _____

ALTAR _____ _____

RECEPTION SITE _____

TIME _____

DESCRIPTION _____

NUMBER OF TABLES _____

DESCRIPTION OF WEDDING

FORMAL/INFORMAL _____

NUMBER OF BRIDAL ATTENDANTS _____

NUMBER OF GROOMSMEN _____

NUMBER OF GUESTS _____

PERSONAL PREFERENCES

FAVORITE COLORS _____

FAVORITE FLOWERS _____

FAVORITE BOUQUETS _____

MISCELLANEOUS _____

_____

_____

_____

THE WEDDING FLOWERS
ITEMIZED WISH LIST

FLOWERS FOR THE WEDDING PARTY

1) BRIDE	TYPE/FLOWERS	NUMBER	COST
❑ Bouquet			
❑ Tossing Bouquet			
❑ Bouquet Alternatives			
❑ Single long-stemmed flower			
❑ Flowers pinned to dress			
❑ Wrist corsage			
❑ Flowers for prayer book or Bible			
❑ Other			
❑ Flowers for the Hair and Veil			
2) BRIDAL ATTENDANTS			
❑ Bouquet for Maid/ Matron of Honor			
❑ Bouquets for Bridemaids			
❑ Flowers for the Hair			
❑ Other			
3) FLOWER GIRL			
❑ Bouquet/Basket of Petals or Flowers			
❑ Flowers for the Hair			
4) GROOM			
❑ Boutonniere			
5) GROOMSMEN			
❑ Best Man's Boutonniere			
❑ Ushers' Boutonnieres			
❑ Ring Bearer's Boutonierre			
6) FAMILY FLOWERS			
❑ Parents/Stepparents of Bride			
❑ Parents/Stepparents of Groom			
❑ Grandmothers and Grandfathers			
7) OTHER SPECIAL GUESTS			
❑			
❑			
SUBTOTAL			

FLOWERS FOR THE CEREMONY

	TYPE/FLOWERS	NUMBER	COST
❑ Entranceway			
❑ Altar			
❑ *Chuppah*			
❑ Pews			
❑ Candles			
❑ Roses for parents			
❑ Aisle runner			
❑ Other			

FLOWERS FOR THE RECEPTION

	TYPE/FLOWERS	NUMBER	COST
❑ Table Centerpieces			
❑ Buffet Tables			
❑ Head Table			
❑ Place Card Table			
❑ Cake Table			
❑ Cake-Topper, Cake Knife			
❑ Mantels			
❑ Stairways			
❑ Entranceways			
❑ Garnish for Serving Platters			
❑ Rest Room			
❑ Other			

GIFT FLOWERS

	TYPE/FLOWERS	NUMBER	COST
❑ Party Hosts			
❑ Out-of-Town Guests			
❑ Weekend Hosts			
❑ Thank-You's to Friends and Helpers			

OTHER POSSIBILITIES

	TYPE/FLOWERS	NUMBER	COST
(Includes Candles, Luminaries, Lighting,			
Balloons, Fabric)			
❑			
❑			
❑			
SUBTOTAL			
TOTAL			

MEETING WITH A FLORIST: WHAT TO BRING

With your pre-planning research complete, you'll be ready for your first appointment with the florist, whether a full-service florist, who can provide soup-to-nuts floral needs in-house, or a floral designer, who generally comes up with a unifying look for your entire wedding, integrating not only flowers into the decor but lighting and textiles as well. Floral designers, unlike florists, generally do not work out of a shop but instead execute concepts by outsourcing jobs.

The more information you provide and the better your research and planning, the more successful your meetings will be. Bring the following items to your meeting with a florist:

1. *Completed wedding flowers itemized wish list.* Be prepared with your estimated floral needs and desires, from personal (those that are carried, worn, or given as gifts) to site needs, including those for the ceremony and reception.
2. *Gown sketches or photographs.* For your gown, your attendants' gowns, and any headgear.
3. *Swatches.* Include those of your gown, your attendant's gowns, and if possible, table linens at the reception. This is an excellent way to match fabrics with complementary flowers. It may be too early to note the color of dress to be worn by mothers, grandmothers, or any other special people to whom you are giving corsages; this information can be delivered, phoned, or faxed later.
4. *Sizes.* If you or any of your attendants are wearing flowers in your hair, you will need to provide head circumferences for wreaths and ask the best way to attach flowers to chignons, twists, or other hairstyles. You should also include information on attendants' height and weight so that bouquets will be neither too big nor too small.
5. *Sketches or photographs* of groom's and ushers' attire.
6. *Other photographs.* Provide examples of decorations or color schemes you particularly like.

FLORIST NAME _____

_____

CHECKLIST OF QUESTIONS
TO ASK WHEN SELECTING A FLORIST

- ❏ May I see your album or portfolio containing any photographs or illustrations of previous weddings for which you have provided flowers? _____

- ❏ Do you offer wedding packages—and if so, what do they include? _____ _____

- ❏ What, exactly, does "full-service" include? Does it cover such extras as flower petals for flower girls, welcome baskets for out-of-town guests, and special floral gifts for helpers, as well as lighting, candles, or fabrics? _____

- ❏ Can you provide an itemized breakdown of prices before the contract is signed?_____

- ❏ Are deliveries and installations included in the contract? How are the flowers delivered, and by whom? Who is responsible, for example, for distributing and fitting boutonnieres and corsages? Will you, the florist, be personally involved with the wedding-day details and distributions? _____

- ❏ Are gratuities included in the contract?_____

- ❏ If the caterer and the florist are not affiliated, ask: Can you meet with my caterer and cake baker to ensure a complementary overall decor? _____

- ❏ Does the contract specify guarantees on freshness and quality? What about substitutions in the event that a requested flower is unavailable at the last minute?_____

- ❏ What is your cancellation policy?_____

- ❏ Can you provide references? _____

FOR THE FLORIST:
DELIVERY AND INSTALLATION

Once you have contracted with a florist, you will need to give him all the pertinent delivery information. Be sure to confirm the delivery times and locations by calling or sending a reminder card containing the following information:

ADDRESSES FOR FLOWER DELIVERY AND INSTALLATION

CEREMONY LOCATION

DATE _____

TIME _____

RECEPTION LOCATION

DATE _____

TIME _____

AFTER THE CELEBRATION:
RECYCLING YOUR FLOWERS

If you have no plans to use your ceremony and reception flowers again, share them!

- Arrange to have them delivered to area nursing homes and hospitals, local charities, or public buildings, such as the town hall.

DELIVER TO _____

ADDRESS _____

CONTACT _____

PHONE NUMBER _____

- Have centerpieces delivered to various loved ones who were unable to attend the wedding, accompanied by a note from you.

DELIVER TO _____

ADDRESS _____

CONTACT _____

PHONE NUMBER _____

TYPES OF BOUQUETS

There are four basic shapes of bouquets:

1. NOSEGAYS. Nosegays are circular, densely arranged flowers, approximately 18 inches in diameter. Within this circle there may be posies, which are petite nosegays made of tiny buds, or tussy-mussies, another type of small nosegay composed of tiny buds carried in Victorian-period silver, cone-shape holders. Tussy-mussies are often made of flowers that have traditional meanings, true to their Victorian origins. Biedermeier nosegays are arranged in rings of flowers, with each ring including only one flower variety. Nosegays can be carried with either long or short gowns.

2. ARM BOUQUETS. Arm bouquets are crescent-shaped arrangements, curved slightly to fit on the arm. Because they are larger than nosegays, they usually are best suited to long gowns.

3. CASCADES. A bouquet that cascades is one that gracefully trails blossoms and/or greens from its base. It can be any shape, from nosegay to tear-shape, and it looks best with a long gown.

4. SPRAYS. Sprays are flowers gathered together in a triangular-shape cluster. Sprays can be carried with either long or short gowns, since they can be of varying sizes.

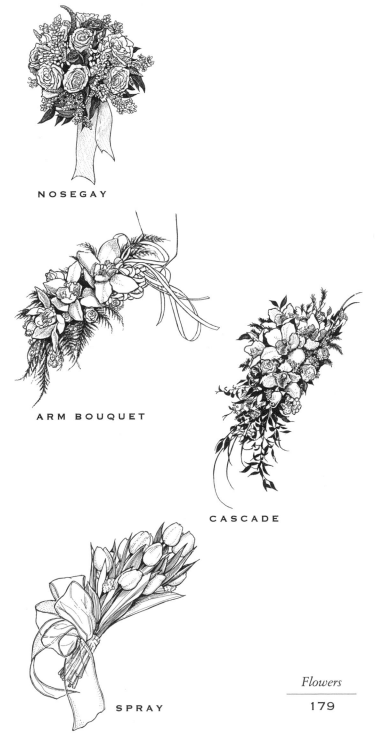

NOSEGAY

ARM BOUQUET

CASCADE

SPRAY

Flowers

179

CHAPTER 14

MUSIC

N o other single element has the power to engage the emotions the way music does. Having music at the ceremony and reception is com-pletely optional, but a choice that most couples agree makes a wonderful day even better. There are myriad ways for the bride and groom to orchestrate and customize their wedding music.

MUSIC: PLANNING AT A GLANCE

- ❏ Find out from your ceremony officiant or in-house music director whether the ceremony site has any restrictions regarding music. Do the same with the reception site manager.
  SIX TO TWELVE MONTHS IN ADVANCE
- ❏ Determine your basic music needs/preferences for both the ceremony and the reception. Consider your budget, the mood you want to create, and your guests' age and taste spectrum.
  SIX TO TWELVE MONTHS IN ADVANCE
- ❏ Ask friends and families for wedding band/musician recommendations; also ask your contacts at both your ceremony and reception sites. Consult wedding magazines, the music departments of local universi-ties, local music shops, and the local musicians union.
  SIX TO TWELVE MONTHS IN ADVANCE
- ❏ Ask to hear singers or instrumentalists live or on tape before you formally reserve their services for the ceremony and/or the reception.
  SIX TO TWELVE MONTHS IN ADVANCE
- ❏ Once you've decided on a reception band, cocktail hour musicians, and/or a DJ, cement the terms of agreement in a written contract. Request that your musicians visit the site sometime before your wedding date so that they are familiar with the setup and acoustics.
  SIX TO TWELVE MONTHS IN ADVANCE
  (CONTINUED)

❏ Meet with your officiant or music director to decide which songs and hymns will be performed during the ceremony.

SIX TO EIGHT MONTHS IN ADVANCE

❏ Discuss with the bandleader or DJ your reception play list, "please don't play" list, announcement needs, and special requests.

TWO TO SIX MONTHS IN ADVANCE, ESPECIALLY IF YOU REQUEST NEW MATERIAL

❏ If you plan a program for the ceremony, include the names of the musicians and soloists, and the musical selections.

TWO TO FOUR WEEKS IN ADVANCE

❏ Call all contracted musicians and soloists to confirm date, time, and site addresses.

ONE TO TWO WEEKS IN ADVANCE

CHECKLIST OF QUESTIONS TO ASK ABOUT THE CEREMONY MUSIC SITE

❏ Does the site have any restrictions regarding music? _____

❏ Must all ceremony music be sacred, or is secular music permitted?

_____

❏ If the ceremony will be held in a place of worship, what musicians and singers are available for weddings, and what are their·fees? _____

❏ What are the size and the acoustics of the ceremony site? (Plot your music needs accordingly.) Can we arrange to hear musicians performing in the space? _____

CHECKLIST OF QUESTIONS TO ASK ABOUT THE RECEPTION MUSIC SITE

❏ Does the site have any restrictions regarding music (such as amplified music or large bands)? _____

❏ Is there a fee for bringing in an outside band? Must the house band be used?_____

❏ What are the size and the acoustics of the reception site? (Plot your music needs accordingly. Just as a big, loud band will overwhelm a small space, a flutist will be barely audible in a vast, cavernous space.) Can we arrange to hear musicians performing in the space? _____

❏ Will microphones and music stands be provided? _____

❏ Does the reception site have a sound system, piano, or stage that we may be interested in using? Are there provisions for prerecorded music? _____

❏ Is there adequate room for the musicians and their equipment to set up adjacent to the dance floor? Does this area have enough electrical outlets to meet our band or DJ's needs? _____

CHECKLIST OF QUESTIONS TO ASK WHEN SELECTING MUSICIANS

FOR A BAND

❏ How many musicians play in the band, and what instruments are represented? How long has this group been together? _____

❏ What type of music is your forte? What is the scope of your repertoire? Are you willing to learn a new song for a wedding, if requested? _____

FOR A DJ

❏ How extensive and varied is your record/CD/tape collection, and how much music will you bring with you? _____

FOR A BAND OR DJ

❏ What is your experience playing at weddings? _____

_____

❏ What is your experience playing at wedding receptions?

_____

❏ Can we get a recent demo tape (audio or video)? Can we make an appointment to hear you in action at a wedding? Will you guarantee that the same musicians, barring emergency, will perform for us? _____

_____

❏ Can we see a list of music that is usually played? _____
❏ What type of equipment do you use? What are your space needs?

_____

❏ Can you (or just the bandleader) visit our reception site prior to the wedding date to familiarize yourself with the setting as it relates to the setup? _____

❏ Are you willing to play special requests? _____
❏ How many breaks (of what length) do you take? Will there be continuous music? _____

❏ What kind of attire do you wear? _____

❏ Will you provide references from recent weddings?

_____

❏ What is your fee? Your cancellation policy? Your payment schedule?
Your overtime charges? _____

_____

MUSICIANS: VITAL INFORMATION

CEREMONY _____

    TIME OF ARRIVAL _____

    TIME OF DEPARTURE _____

RECEPTION _____

    TIME OF ARRIVAL _____

    TIME OF DEPARTURE _____

OTHER _____

    TIME OF ARRIVAL _____

    TIME OF DEPARTURE _____

THE MUSIC PLAY LIST

Start a running list of songs and hymns that have special meaning for you or that you think appropriate for the ceremony and reception. Use the following worksheet to pencil in musical selections:

CEREMONY

- Prelude (reflective background music that begins about 30 minutes prior to the ceremony's start) _____

_____

- Processional (joyous, dramatic music with a slow tempo; the bride may walk down the aisle to the same or different music, played at a higher volume)

_____

_____

- Interludes (during communion, between readings, during lighting of unity candle) _____

_____

- Recessional (often triumphant, majestic, joyous music with a quick tempo)

  _____

  _____

- Postlude (joyous, fast-paced music that is played as guests depart)

  _____

  _____

RECEPTION

- Cocktail hour _____

_____

_____

_____

_____

- The bride and groom's first dance _____
- The bride's dance with her father _____
- The groom's dance with his mother _____
- Dinner music _____

_____

_____

_____

_____

_____

- Dancing music (including any desired ethnic dances or line dances)

_____

_____

_____

_____

_____

- The cake cutting _____
- The bouquet toss and garter toss _____
- Special dedications _____
- Last song _____

A SAMPLING OF MUSICAL SELECTIONS FOR THE CEREMONY AND RECEPTION

WEDDING CEREMONY SONGS

FOR THE PRELUDE

- **Air (Handel)**
- **Rondo (Mozart)**
- **"Jesu Joy of Man's Desiring" (Bach)**
- **Largo (Handel)**
- **Concerto no. 1 (from Vivaldi's *The Four Seasons*, "Spring")**
- **Pavane (Fauré)**

FOR THE PROCESSIONAL

- **The Bridal Chorus (from Wagner's *Lohengrin*)**
- **Wedding March (from Mendelssohn's *A Midsummer Night's Dream*)**
- **"The Prince of Denmark's March" (Clarke)**
- **Wedding March (Guilmant)**
- **Air (Bach)**
- **Canon in D Major (Pachelbel)**
- **"Arrival of the Queen of Sheba" (Handel)**
- **Trumpet Voluntary (Clarke)**
- **Trumpet Tune (Purcell)**

DURING THE CEREMONY

- **"Ave Maria" (Schubert)**
- **"One Hand, One Heart" (Bernstein and Sondheim)**
- **"Jesu Joy of Man's Desiring" (Bach)**
- **"Joyful, Joyful, We Adore Thee" (Beethoven)**
- **"The King of Love My Shepherd" (Hinsworth)**
- **"The Lord's Prayer" (Malotte)**
- **"Biblical Songs" (Dvorák)**
- **"Liebestraum" (Liszt)**
- **"In Thee Is Joy" (Bach)**

FOR THE RECESSIONAL

- **"Ode to Joy" (Beethoven)**
- **Trumpet Voluntary (Clarke)**
- **Wedding March (from Mendelssohn's *A Midsummer Night's Dream*)**
- **Trumpet Tune (Purcell)**

- **Overture** (Handel)
- **Rondeau** (Mouret)
- **"Le Rejouissance"** (Handel)

Popular contemporary selections include "Benedictus" (Simon and Garfunkel), "Wedding Song (There Is Love)" (Noel Paul Stookey), "Evergreen" (Barbra Streisand and Paul Williams), "The Hawaiian Wedding Song" (Andy Williams), and "All I Ask of You" (from *Phantom of the Opera*).

RECEPTION SONGS: SPECIAL DANCES

- **"All I Ask of You"** (from *Phantom of the Opera*)
- **"All I Want Is You"** (U2)
- **"At Last"** (Etta James)
- **"Because You Loved Me"** (Celine Dion)
- **"Can't Help Falling in Love"** (Elvis Presley)
- **"Can You Feel the Love Tonight"** (Elton John, from *The Lion King*)
- **"Cheek to Cheek"** (Tony Bennett)
- **"(Everything I Do) I Do It For You"** (Bryan Adams)
- **"Forever and Ever, Amen"** (Randy Travis)
- **"Have I Told You Lately That I Love You"** (Rod Stewart, Van Morrison)
- **"Heart Full of Love"** (from *Les Misérables*)
- **"Here, There, and Everywhere"** (The Beatles)
- **"If Tomorrow Never Comes"** (Garth Brooks)
- **"I'll Always Love You"** (Taylor Dayne)
- **"I'll Be There"** (Mariah Carey)
- **"In Your Eyes"** (Peter Gabriel)
- **"Isn't It Romantic"** (Frank Sinatra)
- **"Just the Way You Are"** (Billy Joel)
- **"Love Song"** (The Cure)
- **"My Girl"** (The Temptations)
- **"My Heart Belongs to Daddy"** (Cole Porter)
- **"The Power of Love"** (Celine Dion)
- **"Someone Like You"** (Van Morrison)
- **"Stand by Me"** (Ben E. King)
- **"True Companion"** (Marc Cohn)

MUSIC LIST CONTINUES

- "Unchained Melody" (The Righteous Brothers)
- "Unforgettable" (Natalie Cole)
- "What a Wonderful World" (Louis Armstrong)
- "When a Man Loves a Woman" (Percy Sledge)
- "A Whole New World" (Peabo Bryson and Regina Belle, from *Aladdin*)
- "Wind Beneath My Wings" (Bette Midler)
- "Wonderful Tonight" (Eric Clapton)
- "You're My Home" (Billy Joel)
- "You're the Top" (Cole Porter)

RECEPTION: MY SPECIAL REQUESTS

1. _____
2. _____
3. _____
4. _____
5. _____
6. _____
7. _____
8. _____
9. _____
10. _____
11. _____
12. _____
13. _____
14. _____
15. _____
16. _____
17. _____
18. _____

MUSIC COST-CUTTERS

- Go with the musicians provided by your church or synagogue.
- Choose a DJ, typically about half the price of a band.
- Obtain cocktail-hour musicians through the music department of a local university or high school.
- Play prerecorded music during your cocktail hour (having tested it in advance).
- Overlap. Ask one or more multitalented band members to play during the cocktail hour.
- Have a band of fewer pieces.

MUSICIANS COST BREAKDOWN

CEREMONY FEES	COST
ORGANIST	
VOCAL SOLOIST(S)	
INSTRUMENTAL SOLOIST(S)	
RECEPTION FEES	
COCKTAIL-HOUR MUSICIAN(S)	
BAND	
DJ	
EXTRAS, SPECIAL EFFECTS	
OTHER	
GRATUITIES	
DEPOSIT REQUIRED	
CANCELLATION POLICY	
TOTAL	

CHAPTER 15

PHOTOGRAPHY AND
VIDEOGRAPHY

❏ Initiate a search for photographers and videographers who suit your personal needs and preferences. Meet with candidates and review samples of their work before making a decision. Determine your budget for photography and videography.
AT LEAST SIX BUT IDEALLY TWELVE MONTHS IN ADVANCE

❏ Have an engagement photo taken for the newspaper. You can try out one of the photographers you've initially interviewed.
SIX TO TWELVE MONTHS IN ADVANCE

❏ Once you've decided on a photographer and videographer, negotiate the terms of your agreement, and get it all down in a written contract. Write down and give each of them your list of must-have images. SIX TO EIGHT MONTHS IN ADVANCE

❏ Find out your local newspaper's requirements for wedding announcements, and alert your photographer to your needs. ONE TO THREE MONTHS IN ADVANCE

❏ Arrange to have studio portraits taken prior to the wedding date, preferably at your final fitting to save time. APPROXIMATELY ONE MONTH IN ADVANCE

❏ Establish a precise timetable for wedding day portraits. ONE MONTH IN ADVANCE

❏ Assign a friend or two to point out key friends and family members to the photographer and videographer on the day of the wedding.
ONE TO TWO WEEKS IN ADVANCE

❏ Call to reconfirm schedules with photographer and videographer.
ONE TO TWO WEEKS IN ADVANCE

❏ Review proofs and select images for inclusion in album(s) and for enlargements. Make a list of friends and family members who should receive photos or an album of their own. THREE TO FOUR WEEKS AFTER THE WEDDING

❏ Receive completed photography album(s) from photographer.
EIGHT TO TWELVE WEEKS AFTER THE WEDDING

PHOTOGRAPHY SITE CHECKS

- Find out from the site managers of both locations (wedding and reception) whether there are any restrictions on photography/videography. Ask when the photographer can come in and set up equipment and who his contact person at the site will be.
- Request that your photographer and videographer visit your ceremony and reception sites so that they are aware of the settings' lighting requirements and will not have to determine their angles and portrait backdrops at the last minute. Better yet, offer to meet them there, and brainstorm together.
- Don't bank on being able to take group portraits outside on the ceremony site steps. Have indoor backdrops in mind as well, in case of inclement weather.

CHOOSING A PHOTOGRAPHER AND VIDEOGRAPHER

Your wedding photographs and videotapes are a tangible record of a wonderful time in your lives and a gift for generations hence, which makes selecting the right person for the job imperative.

The most telling element of a photographer's background is the work he has done. When you visit a photographer or videographer, ask to see a portfolio or samples of his or her work. If you like what you see, find out whether your schedules are compatible. If so, you can then discuss your needs and estimated costs.

The most important point in interviewing photographers, however, is to feel comfortable with each other. You will want to choose someone with whom you will feel relaxed and open, so that when the big day arrives, you won't feel self-conscious, and the camera won't seem intrusive.

Before you meet with any photographers, consider the style you prefer. Traditional wedding photographs are usually standardized posed shots taken in a studio under controlled lighting. Studio photographers can provide crisp, well-lit images that are technically polished.

Photographers who work in a photojournalistic style place less emphasis on formal posed shots; they look instead to capture the moment and let the picture tell the story. They often shoot both black-and-white and color photographs.

While traditional posed studio shots have long been the mainstay of wedding photography, the photojournalistic approach is becoming more mainstream. Some couples are choosing to use both types of photographers, if their budget allows.

Once you've chosen a photographer, ask him to write up an itemized cost breakdown. Have him include in the contract the date, the agreed-upon arrival time, the length of shooting period, a rough estimate of how many photos will be taken, any extra charges, and a schedule for reviewing proofs and delivery of the finished album.

CHECKLIST OF QUESTIONS TO ASK WHEN SELECTING A PHOTOGRAPHER

PRELIMINARY (ON THE PHONE)

- ❏ Are you available on our wedding date? _____
- ❏ How would you characterize your photography style and philosophy (traditional, portrait-based, photojournalistic)? _____
- ❏ Do you have experience shooting weddings? _____
- ❏ Generally, what kind of wedding photography packages do you offer? Are different levels of service available? _____

IN PERSON

- ❏ May I see recent samples of your own work? (Look at sample books and proofs, including some that show how individual weddings were covered. Are the photos in albums beautifully mounted? Are the images sharp, thoughtfully composed, well lit? Do they effectively capture special emotions, relationships, and moments?) _____
- ❏ Are you familiar with our ceremony and reception sites? Will you visit them prior to the wedding day (especially if this will be your first job at the site)? _____
- ❏ Are you the photographer who will be taking the pictures? Do you work with an assistant? What is his/her role? _____
- ❏ Do you have the capacity to provide digital previewing for use in a private website? _____
- ❏ Can you give us an estimate of how many rolls of film you will use and how many pictures you will take? _____
  _____
- ❏ How much time will you need to take portraits before the ceremony? Between the ceremony and the reception? _____

- ❏ How long will you stay at the reception? What is the charge, if any, for overtime? _____
- ❏ What attire will you wear to the ceremony and reception? _____
- ❏ What is the minimum number of proofs that we will receive? Will they be marked in any way? Will black-and-white proofs be made or just contact sheets? Do we get to keep proofs after selections have been made? _____
- ❏ When can we expect to see proofs? A finished album? Are there any restrictions about the amount of time we have to review proofs and place our order?

  _____
- ❏ What size albums do you use? Can you combine full-page shots with smaller shots in your layout? _____
- ❏ Can we keep the negatives? Will you sell the negatives to us now or in the future? Will you keep the negatives in a fireproof container?

  _____
- ❏ Do you offer a package discount for extra albums for parents and other relatives? _____
- ❏ What is your cancellation policy? Your payment schedule? _____

  _____
- ❏ Will you provide references? (Obtain the list and call them.) _____

  _____

PHOTOGRAPHER'S NAME _____

_____

THE ROMANCE OF BLACK-AND-WHITE

The timeless romance of black-and-white photography is attracting more and more couples who prefer a candid, photojournalistic approach to document their wedding. Black-and-white film is less expensive than color but is more expensive to process and print. Make sure your photographer is skilled in this area and is willing to switch back and forth, capturing, for example, the processional in color and the recessional in black-and-white.

WORKSHEET:
THE PHOTOGRAPHER'S CONTRACT

Get everything in writing. The contract should include the following provisions.

PHOTOGRAPHER/STUDIO _____

CONTRACT DATE _____

CONTRACT COSTS _____

EXTRA CHARGES _____

PRICE GUARANTEES FOR EXTRA PHOTOS, ENLARGEMENTS, ALBUM PAGES,

UPGRADES _____

ANY SUBSTITUTIONS _____

PAYMENT SCHEDULE _____

CANCELLATION POLICY _____

ARRIVAL TIME AT EACH SITE _____

LENGTH OF SHOOTING PERIOD _____

SCHEDULE FOR REVIEWING PROOFS _____

TIME FRAME FOR DELIVERY OF COMPLETED ALBUM(S) _____

CHECKLIST OF QUESTIONS TO ASK
WHEN SELECTING A VIDEOGRAPHER

PRELIMINARY (ON THE PHONE)

❑ Are you available on our wedding date? _____

❑ How would you characterize your videography style and philosophy
(traditional, photojournalistic)? _____

❑ Do you shoot weddings exclusively? If not, what percentage of your
business is weddings? _____

❑ Generally, what kind of wedding videography packages do you offer?
Are different levels of service available? _____

IN PERSON

❑ May we see recent samples of your own work? (Ask to see videos at
each level—unedited, edited in-camera, and edited post-production
with special effects and photo montages. Ask to view a sample of video
footage taken in low-light conditions, such as a church or candlelit

*Photography
and
Videography*

195

reception. Are the videos steady, sharply focused, well lit, and nicely composed? Is the color good and the sound clear, particularly during the vows?) _____

❑ Are you the videographer who will be taking the video? If not, can we arrange to meet that person? Do you work with an assistant? What is his/her role? _____

❑ Will you have backup equipment with you? _____

❑ Do you have the capacity to provide digital previewing for use in a private website? _____

❑ How many videocassettes will you use? _____

❑ Are you familiar with the ceremony and reception sites? If not, are you willing to visit them sometime prior to the wedding date? _____

❑ Will you work from a list of events that we would like to have recorded? _____

❑ How long will you stay at the reception? What is the charge, if any, for overtime? _____

❑ What attire will you wear to the ceremony and reception? _____

❑ Will you be editing the video? What is the difference in price between a video that is edited postproduction or in-camera? _____

❑ When can we expect to see a finished video? _____

❑ Will you coordinate microphone needs with our officiant, and provide us with a cordless microphone(s) to capture our vows? _____

❑ Can you write up an itemized cost breakdown? Will the contract include the agreed-upon arrival time, the length of shooting period, the number of hours of video to be taken, any extra charges, and a schedule for delivery of the edited video? _____

❑ Do you offer a package discount for extra videos for parents and other relatives? For highlights reels? _____

❑ What is your cancellation policy? Your payment schedule? _____

❑ Will you provide references? _____

❑ Are you willing to meet with our still photographer to coordinate strategy? _____

VIDEOGRAPHER'S NAME _____

_____

FIND A PAL WITH A POLAROID

Ask a friend with a Polaroid camera to take some pictures during the reception that you and your mate will be able to take and enjoy on your honeymoon.

CHECKLIST:
THE VIDEOGRAPHER'S CONTRACT

Get everything in writing. The contract should include the following provisions.

PHOTOGRAPHER/STUDIO _____

CONTRACT DATE _____

CONTRACT COSTS _____

EXTRA CHARGES _____

PRICE GUARANTEES FOR EXTRA VIDEOS _____

ANY SUBSTITUTIONS _____

PAYMENT SCHEDULE _____

CANCELLATION POLICY _____

ARRIVAL TIME AT EACH SITE _____

LENGTH OF SHOOTING PERIOD _____

SCHEDULE FOR VIEWING OR DELIVERY OF VIDEO(S) _____

TOSS-AWAY CAMERAS

Placing a flash-equipped disposable camera on each guest table at your reception is a great way to get supplementary candids. Some tips: Look to discount stores and buy in bulk. Don't neglect to factor in the cost of having the film processed and developed. The specially decorated disposable cameras designed for wedding use take just 12 pictures. Ask a friend or family member to collect the cameras shortly before the end of the reception.

PHOTOGRAPHY AND VIDEOGRAPHY COST-CUTTERS

- Look for freelance professional photographers who work out of their homes rather than those who work for a studio. They generally have fewer overhead expenses.
- Hire a photographer who allows you to have smaller multiple images mounted on individual album pages at no extra cost. This lets you choose more photographs for posterity.
- Hire a photographer with Internet savvy. He or she may be willing to save you both money by sidestepping proofs and, instead, transferring images to a private website for you to preview and make selections.
- Contract a photographer who is willing to part with the negatives after your album is made. Then have your additional prints made by a quality discount film processor and developer.
- Arrange with the photographer to have the album made as long as a year afterward, when your funds may not be so depleted.
- Use a professional photographer only for formal portraits and to cover the ceremony. Have shutterbug friends and family take photographs at the reception. (This cost-cutting idea works best for a small wedding.)
- Cut back on the hours of service by your videographer. Have only the ceremony videotaped.
- Choose in-camera editing of your video rather than the more expensive studio editing.
- If a friend or family member who has a quality video camera offers to take footage at the celebrations, take him up on the offer. But do so only if he makes the offer; you can't invite a guest to your wedding and then ask him to work during the festivities.
- Protect your investment by storing your video horizontally, in a box, in a cool, dry place away from sunlight or fluorescent lights.

WISH LIST OF PHOTOS AND VIDEOS

First provide your photographer and videographer with a copy of the sites' photography regulations and restrictions regarding the use of cameras, flash photography, lights, tripods, and sound equipment. Then make a list of must-have images. In the worksheet below, check off which images you'd like the photographer to concentrate on and whether you want to see them in posed or candid style. Supply your videographer with a similar list of events, people to be included, and any people you want interviewed. Remember that it is equally important to let the photographer and videographer know what you don't want.

Ahead of Time

	PHOTO	VIDEO	POSED	CANDID
ENGAGEMENT PHOTO				
FORMAL BRIDAL PORTRAIT				

"Getting Ready" Pictures

If you want work in-progress shots, you might book the photographer to start before the wedding begins, taking pictures as you get ready. These shots could include:

	PHOTO	VIDEO	POSED	CANDID
BRIDE PUTTING ON FINISHING TOUCHES— A NECKLACE OR MAKEUP WITH VEIL				
BRIDE KISSING MOTHER GOOD-BYE AS SHE LEAVES FOR CEREMONY				
BRIDE AND FATHER ARRIVING AT CEREMONY				
OTHERS:				

Ceremony Photographs

Depending on your ceremony site's rules and regulations regarding photography, you may have to re-create certain ceremony photographs in the time between the wedding and the reception. Don't think you have to rerun the entire wedding ceremony to get the right shots. Simply select specific images you want to re-create instead. Otherwise, the process will drag on, and guests will be left with an overload of downtime between the wedding and the reception. Possible ceremony photos would include:

	PHOTO	VIDEO	POSED	CANDID
BRIDE AND FATHER WALKING UP AISLE				
BRIDESMAIDS, MAID OF HONOR, FLOWER GIRL, AND RING BEARER WALKING UP AISLE				
GROOM AND BEST MAN TURNED TO WATCH BRIDE WALK UP AISLE				
BRIDE AND GROOM STANDING OR KNEELING AT ALTAR AND/OR EXCHANGING VOWS (CAN BE RE-CREATED FOR PHOTO)				
BRIDE, GROOM, AND THEIR CHILDREN AT ALTAR ENTIRE WEDDING PARTY AT ALTAR				
BRIDE AND GROOM KISSING				
BRIDE AND GROOM RECESSIONAL				
OTHER				

Reception Photographs

There are three kinds of reception photographs:

1. Posed portraits of the wedding party and family members with the bride and groom.
2. Shots of planned events, such as cake-cutting, first dances, and bouquet-tossing.
3. Candid photos of everyone at the reception as it progresses.

Portraits

Posing for pictures with your respective families can get a little complicated these days. If your parents are divorced, it is simply not appropriate to ask them to flank you in a photograph in a semblance of a united family. Instead, a portrait of you with each of them individually is fine—and if they have remarried, have a portrait taken of you with each of them and their spouse. Possible formal shots might be:

	PHOTO	VIDEO	POSED	CANDID
BRIDE ALONE				
GROOM ALONE				
BRIDE AND GROOM TOGETHER				
BRIDE AND MAID/MATRON OF HONOR				
BRIDE WITH HER PARENTS (OR EACH PARENT, PLUS STEPPARENT)				
GROOM WITH HIS PARENTS (OR EACH PARENT, PLUS STEPPARENT)				
GROOM AND BEST MAN				
BRIDE WITH HER MOTHER				
BRIDE WITH HER FATHER				
GROOM WITH HIS MOTHER				
GROOM WITH HIS FATHER				

Portraits (continued)

	PHOTO	VIDEO	POSED	CANDID
BRIDE AND GROOM WITH ALL ATTENDANTS				
BRIDE WITH HER ATTENDANTS				
GROOM WITH HIS ATTENDANTS				
BRIDE AND GROOM WITH HER FAMILY (PARENTS, SIBLINGS, AUNTS, UNCLES, COUSINS)				
BRIDE AND GROOM WITH HIS FAMILY (PARENTS, SIBLINGS, AUNTS, UNCLES, COUSINS)				
BRIDE AND GROOM WITH THEIR SIBLINGS, IF NOT ALL IN WEDDING PARTY				
BRIDE WITH "GENERATIONS" (HER PARENTS AND GRANDPARENTS)				
GROOM WITH HIS PARENTS AND GRANDPARENTS				
OTHERS				

Planned Events

For planned events—both the traditional ones, such as the cake-cutting, and those that personalize your wedding—ask an attendant, close friend, or even the catering manager to direct the photographer to the site of each so that he can be thinking in advance about the best way to frame the scene. Planned events can include:

	PHOTO	VIDEO	POSED	CANDID
BRIDE AND GROOM ARRIVING AT RECEPTION				
GUESTS ON RECEIVING LINE				
CLOSE-UPS OF CAKE TABLE, CENTERPIECES, OTHER SPECIAL DECORATIONS				
BEST MAN TOASTING BRIDE AND GROOM				
BRIDE AND GROOM CUTTING CAKE				
BRIDE AND GROOM FEEDING EACH OTHER CAKE				
GROOM TOASTING THE BRIDE				
BRIDE AND GROOM'S FIRST DANCE				
BRIDE DANCING WITH HER FATHER				
GROOM DANCING WITH HIS MOTHER				
BRIDE TOSSING BOUQUET				
GROOM TOSSING BRIDE'S GARTER				
BRIDE AND GROOM LEAVING RECEPTION				
OTHERS				

NAMES OF NOT-TO-BE-MISSED GUESTS

(Delegate a friend or relative to point out these VIPs to your photographer and videographer.)

_____

_____

_____

_____

FORMAL STUDIO PORTRAITS: VITAL INFORMATION

PLACE _____

DATE _____

TIME _____

WHAT TO BRING _____

_____

_____

PEOPLE TO NOTIFY _____

_____

_____

DISPLAY AT RECEPTION? _____

PERSON RESPONSIBLE _____

DAY RATES VERSUS NUMBER OF PHOTOS

Many photographers charge a day rate or creative fee that incorporates their services for an allotted time and a minimum number of proofs or rolls of film shot. A day rate might also include one or more of the following elements: an engagement shoot, a bridal portrait, a standard album with a predetermined number of prints, a set number of enlargements, a full set of (ideally unmarked) proofs, and a black-and-white glossy for the newspaper.

PHOTOGRAPHY COST BREAKDOWN

ITEM	COST OF EACH	TOTAL COST	DEPOSIT	BALANCE DUE
ENGAGEMENT SHOOT				
PRINTS				
FORMAL STUDIO SHOOT				
PHOTOGRAPHER'S DAY RATE				
SECOND PHOTOGRAPHER				
ASSISTANT				
EXTRAS (E.G., B&W PIX)				
WEDDING ALBUM				
EXTRA PRINTS/PAGES				
UPGRADES				
PARENTS' ALBUMS				
EXTRA PRINTS/PAGES				
UPGRADES				
ADDITIONAL PRINTS				
COLOR				
___ 4 X 6S @ $				
___ 5 X 7S @ $				
___ 8 X 10S @ $				
BLACK-AND-WHITE				
___ 4 X 6S @ $				
___ 5 X 7S @ $				
___ 8 X 10S @ $				
NEGATIVES BUYOUT				
OTHER				
OVERTIME CHARGE				
TRANSPORTATION/PARKING				
MEAL				
CANCELLATION POLICY				
TOTAL				

VIDEOGRAPHY COST BREAKDOWN

ITEM	COST OF EACH	TOTAL COST	DEPOSIT	BALANCE DUE
VIDEOGRAPHER'S FEE				
SECOND VIDEOGRAPHER				
ASSISTANT				
UNEDITED TAPE(S)				
VIDEO EDITED IN-CAMERA				
VIDEO POST-EDITED				
PHOTO MONTAGE				
HIGHLIGHTS				
SPECIAL EFFECTS				
MUSIC				
ADDITIONAL TAPE				
OTHER				
OVERTIME CHARGE				
TRANSPORTATION/ PARKING				
MEAL				
CANCELLATION POLICY				
TOTAL				

SPECIAL EFFECTS

Many videographers offer a range of special frills and effects. Background music, appropriate to the occasion and even scene-specific, is one option; decorative frames and photo montages are others. Some videographers will even do a introductory photo montage of the bride and groom's childhoods; all that the two of you have to provide are the photographs.

PICTURES FOR POSTERITY

For posterity's sake, ask to have your wedding photographs mounted in photography albums containing archival, acid-free paper for acid-free preservation.

INSTANT PHOTO ALBUMS: DIGITAL CAMERAS AND WEBSITES

Services such as E-Prints (www.e-prints.com) and Memories Online (www.memoriesonline.com) enable photographers to promptly post wedding pictures on a private website for online previewing by newlyweds and their families. Guests can access the site by typing in an Internet address. Your photographer may register with a service or create his own. A digital camera makes it easier to transfer images to the Internet. If the convenience of an online picture preview and wedding album is important to you, be sure to find out whether the photographer owns a digital camera before booking him.

CHAPTER 16

THE WEDDING CAKE

T he wedding cake is not an insignificant part of the wedding budget. Wedding cakes can cost anywhere from $200 up to several thousand dollars and are often priced on a flat fee or on a per-slice basis, ranging any- where from $1 to $20 a serving. Some hotels and reception halls even tack on a per-serving cutting fee if your cake was not made by the onsite baker. But for many couples, a wedding cake is an item worth splurging on—as a striking symbol of the marriage union, a beautifully adorned temple of nuptial bliss.

THE WEDDING CAKE: PLANNING AT A GLANCE

❏ Get recommendations from friends. Make an appointment to meet and review any baker's portfolio, whether he is the baker at the club, the one used by the caterer, or one you find yourself. Ask to see photographs of the baker's work. You'll want your cake to look good, but looks aren't everything—you'll want it to taste good, too. Most reputable bakers offer tastings of cakes, fillings, and icing. Always sample a baker's work before signing a contract. Check the baker's references. THREE TO SIX MONTHS AHEAD, ALTHOUGH SOME SPECIALTY BAKERS MAY NEED A YEAR IN ADVANCE IF YOU'RE PLANNING A JUNE WEDDING

❏ Nail down the terms of your agreement—size, tiers, flavors, ingredients, decorations, presentation, delivery date, time, location, and directions—in a written contract. THREE MONTHS AHEAD

❏ Provide the baker with the names and phone numbers of the reception site manager or caterer, your wedding planner, and especially important if the cake will be decorated with edible flowers—your florist to coordinate details and delivery. ONE TO THREE MONTHS AHEAD

❏ Confirm with your caterer how the cake will be plated. ONE MONTH AHEAD

❏ Confirm cake delivery arrangements and directions to the reception site with both the baker and the site manager or caterer. ONE TO TWO WEEKS AHEAD

WHO BAKES THE WEDDING CAKE?

Your wedding cake may be ordered from the caterer, a restaurant, the reception site, a professional bakery, a grocery bakery, or a master baker. If the wedding is small, a friend who is a skillful baker may offer to make your wedding cake.

FACTORS TO CONSIDER WHEN CHOOSING A CAKE

- Your budget
- The formality of your wedding
- Whether the reception site requires that you use an in-house cake or pay an additional fee to bring one from the outside
- The reception menu
- The inclusion of other desserts

CHECKLIST OF QUESTIONS TO ASK WHEN SELECTING A BAKER

❏ Will this be a fresh-baked cake, or will it be a previously frozen cake? _____

❏ What size cake is right for the number of guests we expect? _____

❏ What combinations of flavors of cake, filling, and icing are available? Which do customers most often request? _____

❏ What decorative options do you offer? Will you work from a photograph? Can you customize my cake? _____

❏ Do you make groom's cakes? _____

❏ What is the price range for your cakes? What factors determine the costs? _____

❏ What Can we have a smaller cake than we need and supplement it with a less expensive sheet cake in the kitchen? _____

❏ What is the last day that we may make any changes to our order (number of people or design)? _____

❏ Will there be an additional charge for delivery? _____

❏ Is a deposit required? Is there a charge or deposit required for cake stands and pillars? _____

❏ Are deposits refundable? _____

❏ When is the final payment due? _____

❏ What is your cancellation policy? _____

BAKER _____

CAKE DELIVERY DATE _____

TIPS ON PLANNING
THE WEDDING CAKE

- You'll want to order your wedding cake at least six to eight weeks in advance. If yours is a limited engagement period or a last-minute nuptial, you can get good-quality cakes at short notice from professional bakeries and grocery-store deli bakeries.

- Does the reception site require that you use a cake provided by the in-house caterer or charge a cake-cutting fee for cakes baked by an off-site baker?

- Work with your baker to choose a cake texture and icing that blend flavors nicely.

- If your cake is to be baked at another site and transported, it is a good idea to follow up yourself and tell the site caterer or club manager when the cake will be delivered. A cake consisting of more than three tiers is generally transported unassembled and put together and decorated on site. Find out from the location manager if there is space for the baker to work and the best time for him or her to do so.

- Be careful using fresh flowers. Some, such as foxglove, larkspur, and monk's hood, are known to be poisonous. As a general rule, avoid having any real flowers touch the frosting, and avoid putting stems into the cake.

BRING ON THE HEIRLOOMS

Your family may have passed down through the years some handsome heirloom cake stands or cake knives—even heirloom cake toppers—whose inclusion you wouldn't dream of omitting at your wedding reception. Be sure to let the baker know of your wishes in the planning stages, so he can design a cake that will complement your heirlooms.

THE BAKER NEEDS TO KNOW

When choosing a wedding cake, give the baker the specifics regarding the size and type of wedding you are planning. Include the particulars of the reception, such as:

- Number of Guests Expected _____
- Additional Dessert Plans _____
- Season and Temperature _____
- Room Decor _____
- Ceiling Height _____
- Kitchen Details (e.g., refrigerator) _____
- Linen Colors _____
- Wedding Party Colors _____
- Floral Scheme (Flower Types and Colors) _____

Also provide the baker with:

- The names and numbers of your other vendors, including the caterer, florist, and wedding planner.
- The name and number of the reception site location manager to coordinate details and delivery.
- Clear directions to the reception site. If necessary, drive the route between the bakery and the reception site yourself to ensure that your directions make sense.

GROOM'S CAKE

Having a second cake, called a groom's cake, at your reception is a charming touch. The groom's cake was traditionally a dark fruitcake, contrasting with the white fruitcake wedding cake. Today the groom's cake is often a chocolate cake that is iced in chocolate; it might also be baked in a shape, such as a football or a book, that reflects an interest of the groom. If it is to be used as a second dessert, it is placed on a separate table from the wedding cake and cut and served by the staff. At a small, at-home wedding, it may be cut and served when the wedding cake is served.

CAKE VOCABULARY

You don't know the difference between a marzipan paste and a fondant finish? Here's a primer on some of the terms you will be discussing with your baker.

BUTTERCREAM

- Buttercream is smooth and creamy—but not too sweet.
- It takes flavors well, remains soft so that it is easy to cut, and is perfect for finishes such as basketweaves, swags and swirls, fleur-de-lis, and rosettes.
- Genuine buttercream is made with real butter, so cakes iced with buttercream need to be kept in a cool place; heat and humidity make it bead, run, and drip. Some bakers counter this effect by adding shortening to the icing to give it a measure of stability. If your cake will be kept cool in an air-conditioned reception room, the added shortening is unnecessary. If you demand true, all-butter icing, ask the baker to forego shortening altogether.
- Cakes iced in buttercream are the best value in terms of price per slice.

WHIPPED CREAM

- Whipped cream is a light, soft icing that, as with buttercream, becomes temperamental in heat and humidity.
- A whipped-cream cake must be kept refrigerated until just before it is served. Bakers may also use stabilizers when working with whipped cream. If you don't want stabilizers used, discuss with your baker whether this will affect the appearance of the cake.

FONDANT

- Rolled fondant icing is a combination of sugar, corn syrup, gelatin, and usually glycerin.
- Fondant can be rolled out in sheets and wrapped around each tier of the cake, presenting a smooth frosting with a porcelain-like sheen.
- Fondant serves as the perfect base for flowers and decorations piped in royal icing (see next page) because of its smoothness.
- A cake iced in fondant cannot be refrigerated. While this is not a problem for the cake, it may be for a filling that requires refrigeration.

ROYAL ICING

- Soft when it is piped onto a cake, royal icing dries to a hard finish.
- Bakers use royal icing for creating latticework, flowers, and beading around the edges of the cake. It is used for decorative touches only, not to ice an entire cake.

SPUN SUGAR, PASTILLAGE, AND MARZIPAN

- Finishing touches can be made using any of these decorative icings, all of which are edible.
- Spun sugar is caramelized sugar that is pulled into strands and quickly formed into bows and other shapes. It melts into a gooey mess in heat and humidity, so it isn't a good choice for a room without air-conditioning.
- Pastillage is a paste of sugar, cornstarch, and gelatin that hardens as it dries to a porcelain-like finish. It is used to create realistic-looking flowers and decorations.
- Marzipan is also a paste, made of ground almonds, sugar, and egg whites. It is sometimes rolled in sheets, as with fondant, but it is usually molded into flowers and other decorative shapes and painted with food coloring.

TIPS ON CAKE TOPPERS

Cake toppers are an art form all their own these days. They may be created from ceramics, porcelain, hand-blown glass, plastic, clay—even crocheted from yarn.

- Make sure your choice of cake topper marries nicely with the design of the cake. You want the topper to complement, not clash with, the cake. A tiny plastic model of the car you drove on your first date, for example, may detract from an elegant-looking cake.
- If you decide to use confectionery flowers as a cake topper, be sure to discuss the choice of flowers first with your florist. You'll want your flowers to complement the wedding's floral scheme.
- Ask your baker for recommendations for cake toppers. He may be able to suggest the perfect choice to match his cake design.

WEDDING CAKE DELIVERY AND INSTALLATION

Once you have contracted with a baker, you will need to give him all the pertinent delivery information. Be sure to confirm the delivery times and locations by calling or sending a reminder card containing the following information:

CAKE DELIVERY AND INSTALLATION

RECEPTION LOCATION _____

DATE _____

TIME _____

THE TRADITIONAL CUTTING OF THE CAKE

The cutting of the first slice of wedding cake by the bride and groom remains a popular reception event. As such, there is a proper way to do it.

- To start, the bride puts her hand on the handle of the cake knife and the groom puts his hand over hers.
- Pierce the bottom tier of the cake with the point of the knife and then carefully make three cuts (two sides and one end), removing a small slice onto a plate provided by the caterer in advance, along with two forks.
- The groom gently feeds the bride the first bite, and she feeds him the second.

CUTTING THE ENTIRE CAKE

If the wedding is small or at home, you'll want someone to be in charge of cake-cutting once the two of you have made the traditional first cuts.

Here, then, is a review of the art of cake-cutting:

1. Start by cutting the bottom layer. Run a knife all the way around the base of the second layer; the cut runs in a circle parallel to the outside of the bottom layer.
2. Cut individual slices from the bottom layer. Slices are lifted onto cake plates to be served to guests.
3. Next, cut the second layer into individual slices the same way by running the knife all the way around the base of the next layer.
4. Cut individual slices and serve.
5. Next, cut the bottom layer again by running the knife all the way around the base of the second layer; the cut runs in a circle parallel to the outside of the bottom layer.
6. Cut and serve individual slices.
7. Remove the top layer to either cut and serve or freeze and save.

Finally, separate remaining layers to cut and serve.

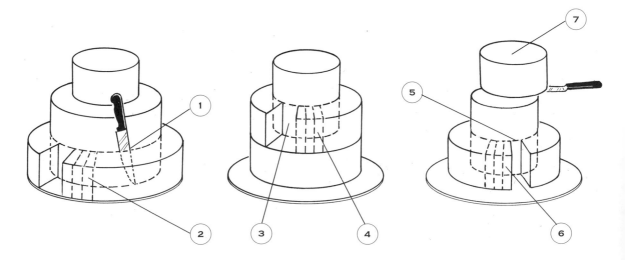

WEDDING CAKE COST BREAKDOWN

ONSITE BAKER		OFF-SITE BAKER	
CAKE	_____	CAKE	_____
COST PER SERVING	_____	COST PER SERVING	_____
CAKE TOPPER	_____	CAKE TOPPER	_____
DELIVERY COST	_____	DELIVERY COST	_____
GROOM'S CAKE	_____	GROOM'S CAKE	_____
OTHER	_____	OTHER	_____
TAX	_____	TAX	_____
TOTAL	▬▬▬	**TOTAL**	▬▬▬

WEDDING CAKE COST-CUTTERS

- WASTE NOT. Many people love big, extravagant wedding cakes, but often much of the cake at a reception goes uneaten. Because cake is generally bought on a per-serving basis, many caterers suggest that you do not order a piece of wedding cake for each of the guests at the reception, unless yours is a sit-down dinner. Buy less: Consider, say, for 300 reception guests, ordering a cake that will feed 225. It will save you quite a bit of money, and you will probably still have leftover cake.
- FAKE CAKE. A good budget-extender is a fake wedding cake with Styrofoam layers. It can be as large as a real cake but cost only a fraction what the real cake would cost. Make the top layer real to freeze for your first anniversary. The whole "cake," frosted beautifully and decorated with fresh flowers, is then carted to the kitchen after you make the first slice in the top layer. Waiters then serve a less-expensive frosted sheet cake to the reception guests.
- FAKE TIERS. If you love the look of a multi-tiered cake, you can have the bottom tiers made of Styrofoam and the top tiers real cake.
- DISPLAY CAKE. Have your baker make a small, elegant cake for display and serve guests slices of a less-expensive sheet cake. The sheet cake should be cut discreetly by the staff in the kitchen and served individually or placed on the cake table for guests to pick up.

CHAPTER 17

HONEYMOON PLANS

The honeymoon is the ultimate indulgence, a romantic interlude bridging your past and future lives. Whether this brief period sees you lying on a sugary white-sand beach or dining in a candlelit hotel room in your own hometown, it is a time to revel in your nuptial bliss—and to recuperate from the hectic planning of the weeks and months before.

THE HONEYMOON: PLANNING AT A GLANCE

❏ Start doing your research as early as possible. You and your intended can find travel information and brochures at travel agencies, on the Internet, in magazines, or at the public library. Ask friends and family for recommendations.

AS SOON AS YOU BECOME ENGAGED

❏ Decide on your honeymoon destination.

FOUR TO TEN MONTHS IN ADVANCE

❏ Make reservations for transportation, lodging, and any tours, restaurants, and activities. Pay necessary deposits on lodging.

FOUR TO TEN MONTHS IN ADVANCE

❏ Start planning your wardrobe, luggage, and accessories.

TWO TO FOUR MONTHS IN ADVANCE

❏ For international travel, obtain passports, visas, and inoculations as necessary.

ONE TO TWO MONTHS IN ADVANCE

❏ Reconfirm all reservations and any plans for ground transportation.

ONE TO TWO WEEKS IN ADVANCE

START PLANNING!

Because the honeymoon is as much the groom's vacation as it is the bride's, the planning should be shared by both of you. That includes doing research, meeting with travel agents, and making reservations.

WHAT KIND OF HONEYMOON?

Honeymoons are big business these days, and the world is your oyster. Tours are available for almost every type of vacation. Just as there are theme weddings, so may honeymoons be planned around a certain activity. Examples of activities, if you are inclined toward a certain type of trip, include:

- Sports/adventure
- Golf or tennis
- Scuba diving or fishing
- Walking or cycling tours
- White-water rafting
- Sailing
- Safaris
- Skiing

- Culture
- Museum tours
- Castle stays
- Luxury train trips
- Culinary
- Wine tours
- Back-roads
- Food rests

The most important issue to consider when planning a honeymoon is finding a spot with activities to please both of you. As fond as you are of each other, you probably don't need to spend every waking hour together. One of you may want to shop around on a lazy afternoon while the other tours a local museum; this will give you lots to talk about later.

HONEYMOON ABROAD: BARE NECESSITIES CHECKLIST

Traveling outside the United States often requires additional paperwork and survival necessities. The following is a general checklist for items you may need when honeymooning on an international scale.

- ❏ PASSPORT/VISA
- ❏ INOCULATIONS
- ❏ PHOTO I.D.
- ❏ ADAPTER FOR SMALL APPLIANCES
- ❏ PRESCRIPTION MEDICATION AND BIRTH CONTROL
- ❏ EXTRA EYEGLASSES OR CONTACT LENSES
- ❏ HEALTH INSURANCE CARD
- ❏ SEPARATE LIST OF CREDIT CARD AND TRAVELER'S CHECKS NUMBERS
- ❏ FIRST-AID KIT
- ❏ ESSENTIAL TOILETRIES

TRAVEL AGENT OR DO-IT-YOURSELF?

There are many advantages to using a travel agent for your honeymoon planning—saving time, for one. The busy couple may find it easier and more efficient to let someone who is knowledgeable in the travel business find and coordinate transportation, accommodations, and transfers. Saving money is another advantage. Travel agents will be able to inform you of all-inclusive honeymoon packages, tours that often include the works—transportation, accommodations, meals, transfers, even cocktails—at attractive prices. Plus you don't pay travel agents a fee for their services; they earn their commission from the airlines, hotels, cruise lines, and tour operators.

Many travel agents even specialize in customized honeymoon vacations and will tailor the trip to meet your personal needs and desires.

On the other hand, seasoned travelers may prefer to do their own plotting and planning. The advantages: You'll have firsthand information on exactly what to expect, and you can customize the trip around your own personal preferences.

However you do the planning, keep in mind the following:

- Make sure the transportation to get to and from your destination is available before you make a deposit or prepay the lodging expenses. You don't want to make a deposit only to find that flights are sold out or the cost to get there is prohibitive.
- Ask about cancellation policies and how late you can cancel your accommodation reservations without losing some or all of your deposit. Get the cancellation policies in writing for tours or hotels.
- Consider the time of your wedding when making airplane reservations. Most likely, you won't feel like taking an early-morning flight the day after an afternoon or evening wedding.
- Honeymooners are often treated as special guests who receive extra amenities. It can't hurt to tell the travel agent or hotel reservationist that you are planning a honeymoon.
- Make sure you ask for a double or queen-size bed in a room in a quiet location.
- If you've done research on local restaurants, you may want to make reservations at the better known eateries prior to your honeymoon, particularly if you will be staying at a popular destination in the high season. You'll also want to book reservations for special tours and activities (tee times, for example, or theater tickets) at busy places.

Honeymoon Plans

221

THE HONEYMOON FACTS

DESTINATION _____

DATE OF DEPARTURE _____

TIME OF DEPARTURE/ARRIVAL _____

FLIGHT/TRAIN/SHIP # _____

TRANSFER TIME OF DEPARTURE/ARRIVAL _____

TRANSFER FLIGHT/TRAIN/SHIP # _____

CAR RENTAL _____

DATES _____

CONFIRMATION # _____

ACCOMMODATION #1 _____

DATES _____

CONFIRMATION # _____

ACCOMMODATION #2 _____

DATES _____

CONFIRMATION # _____

DATE OF RETURN _____

TIME OF RETURN/ARRIVAL _____

FLIGHT/TRAIN/SHIP # _____

TRANSFER TIME _____

TRANSFER FLIGHT/TRAIN/SHIP # _____

THE HOT SPOTS

The most popular honeymoon destinations these days are:

- The Caribbean (St. Thomas, Aruba, Jamaica) and the Bahamas
- Hawaii
- Florida (Orlando/Disney World)
- The Pocono Mountains
- Mexico (Cancun)

DON'T FORGET THE SUNSCREEN: HONEYMOON PACKING CHECKLIST

Your dream trip to a remote tropical island can turn into a nightmare if you forget to pack the toothpaste or some other bare necessity. Check before you leave to see whether the place you are staying has such essentials as shampoo, conditioner, and soap. Many hotels have hair dryers and irons on hand as well, freeing up your suitcase even more. It's a good idea to pack wrinkle-resistant clothing made from some of the new fiber blends. Use the following checklist when packing for your honeymoon:

	BRIDE	GROOM
CLOTHES		
PANTS	❏	❏
SHIRT	❏	❏
DRESS	❏	❏
SWEATER	❏	❏
JACKET	❏	❏
UNDERWEAR	❏	❏
SOCKS/HOSIERY	❏	❏
SPORTS SHOES	❏	❏
DRESSY SHOES	❏	❏
RAIN GEAR	❏	❏
OTHER	❏	❏
_____	❏	❏
_____	❏	❏
TOILETRIES		
BODY LOTION	❏	❏
BRUSH/COMB	❏	❏
DENTAL FLOSS	❏	❏
DEODORANT	❏	❏
FACE CREAM	❏	❏
RAZOR	❏	❏

	BRIDE	GROOM
SOAP	❏	❏
SHAMPOO/CONDITIONER	❏	❏
TOOTHBRUSH/TOOTHPASTE	❏	❏

NECESSITIES

	BRIDE	GROOM
EXTRA PRESCRIPTION GLASSES/CONTACTS	❏	❏
SUNGLASSES	❏	❏
PRESCRIPTION DRUGS	❏	❏
VITAMINS	❏	❏
BIRTH CONTROL	❏	❏
SUNSCREEN	❏	❏
MINI SEWING KIT	❏	❏
CORKSCREW	❏	❏
SPORTS EQUIPMENT (TENNIS RACKET, ETC.)	❏	❏
TRAVELER'S CHECKS/PASSPORT	❏	❏

FIRST AID

	BRIDE	GROOM
ANTACID	❏	❏
ANTISEPTIC	❏	❏
DIARRHEA MEDICATION	❏	❏
BANDAGES	❏	❏
CORTISONE CREAM	❏	❏
ASPIRIN	❏	❏

WHILE YOU'RE AWAY: MAKING ARRANGEMENTS FOR PETS, PLANTS, MAIL, CHILDREN, AND HOME

Planning a honeymoon includes making arrangements so that all you leave behind runs smoothly without you—especially if you have children or own pets. Be sure to leave a written schedule of your trip, including telephone numbers, with the people who are responsible for maintaining any aspect of your home life while you're away. In the spaces below, write down their names and phone numbers. Be sure to take the information with you on your trip.

BABY-SITTER _____

PHONE NUMBER _____

HOUSE-SITTER _____

PHONE NUMBER _____

OFFICE/WORKPLACE CHECK-IN OR MESSAGE NUMBERS _____

Make sure you have determined a method for handling your messages.

BRIDE'S MESSAGE NUMBER _____

GROOM'S MESSAGE NUMBER _____

CRUISING IT

Honeymoon cruises are extremely popular, and for good reason: You have the romance of a ship at sea, scenic destination stops, and a wide range of onboard activities and amenities—all or most of it paid for in advance. (You also leave the driving to someone else!) Cruises can also be attractively priced, with all-inclusive honeymoon packages offered on most cruise lines. If you're looking to cruise it for your honeymoon, be sure to:

- Book with a cruise-only agency or a travel agency that advertises as cruise specialists. Cruise agencies buy large numbers of cruise space at deep discounts and pass the savings to you. Cruise specialists also have insider know-how on cruises.
- Book early. The deeply discounted spaces, much like cheap airfare seats, fill up early.
- If you're booking a package deal, find out whether gratuities and beverages are included. If not, factor these into your total cruise costs.
- Compare cruise lines and rates before committing to one. Inquire about the size of the ship and the number of passengers it holds, as well as the crew-to-passenger ratio (a 2-to-1 ratio, for example, is excellent).
- Shop around for a ship that has the activities and amenities you like.
- Ask about the degree of formality on the ship. Some ships have a dress code for dinner seatings.

HONEYMOON COSTS BREAKDOWN

A LA CARTE

TRANSPORTATION _____

AIR, TRAIN, BUS, CAR _____

TRANSFERS _____

TAXIS _____

TIPS _____

LODGING _____

HOTEL/MOTEL/INN DAY RATE _____

RESORT _____

CONDO _____

MEALS _____

DINNER _____

LUNCH _____

BREAKFAST _____

SNACKS _____

BEVERAGES _____

TIPS _____

ACTIVITIES/ENTERTAINMENT _____

SHOPPING _____

SOUVENIRS _____

TOURS _____

SPORTS _____

MUSIC/MOVIES/THEATER/CLUBS _____

PACKAGE

ALL-INCLUSIVE ROOM, MEALS, TRANSFERS _____

AIR, TRAIN, SHIP, CAR _____

ACTIVITIES/ENTERTAINMENT _____

EXTRA MEALS _____

TOTAL _____

HONEYMOON COST-CUTTERS

Ahoneymoon is a time to celebrate wedded bliss and to splurge. Even so, because the honeymoon is generally funded by the two of you, you may need to find ways to cut costs so that you both can enjoy yourselves without going into debt on your first joint purchase. Here are a few tips:

- Marry in the off-season so that you can have your wedding and honeymoon for considerably discounted prices. The off-season in the Caribbean, for example, is the summer, when hotel and resort rooms can be reserved at bargain prices. In Europe, the off-seasons are generally spring and fall.
- Match the month of your wedding with the seasonality of your honeymoon destination. If your dream is to honeymoon in Barbados, where high season is during the winter months, save on costs by marrying at another time. (Speaking of the Caribbean, you will likely find bargains there during two of the most popular months to marry: September and early October are high season for hurricanes and tropical storms, and many tourists refrain from traveling to the islands during that time.)
- Start planning far enough in advance so that you can shop around for the best prices for the trip you want.
- Whether you're checking on airfares or room costs, always ask if the rate offered is the lowest rate available. If you're flying, ask about advanced-purchase fares, which are based on travel during certain days and times; by coming back a day later or in the morning instead of the evening, for example, you may reap big savings.
- Often you can get a better rate on a hotel room by calling the hotel directly rather than the 800 number. Your travel agent or tour operator also might have lower, blocked-space rates.
- Looking for airfare bargains? Contact a consolidator, who buys up blocks of tickets and offers them at bargain prices.
- Compromise when you can. Fly coach class so that you can stay in a first-class hotel. Or, instead of flying, drive.
- Choose to stay in a condominium or private home; they are generally less expensive than hotels and usually charge by the week rather than by the night. The privacy factor can be greater as well.
- Ask for a room with a kitchen so that you don't have to pay inflated restaurant prices for every meal.
- All-inclusive package deals can often offer the best prices.

CHAPTER 18

THE FINAL FEW WEEKS

I n the last few weeks before your wedding day, with all your major decisions made and set into motion, it's time to complete the details of your plans.

ANNOUNCEMENTS

- **WEDDING ANNOUNCEMENTS**. If you are sending out wedding announcements, address and stamp them and arrange for a relative or friend to put them in the mail on the day after the wedding.
- **NEWSPAPER ANNOUNCEMENTS**. Choose the wedding portrait you want to place in the newspaper and mail it, along with the written announcement, two weeks before the wedding. Check beforehand to see whether the newspaper has any specific requirements for wedding announcement information or even has its own wedding-announcement form to fill out. You may want to enlist the help of the bridal-salon salesperson who sold you your wedding gown or the seamstress who made it for a detailed description to give to the newspaper. In the checklist below keep track of any pertinent information to go into the announcement.

NEWSPAPER ANNOUNCEMENT: PERTINENT INFORMATION

CEREMONY

- ❏ DATE: _____
- ❏ SITE: _____
- ❏ TOWN, STATE: _____
- ❏ OFFICIANT: _____

BRIDE

❏ **FULL NAME:** _____

❏ OCCUPATION: _____

❏ AGE (OPTIONAL): _____

❏ UNIVERSITY/SCHOOL: _____

❏ DEGREE: _____

GROOM

❏ **FULL NAME:** _____

❏ OCCUPATION: _____

❏ AGE (OPTIONAL): _____

❏ UNIVERSITY/SCHOOL: _____

❏ DEGREE: _____

BRIDE'S PARENTS/STEPPARENTS

❏ **NAME:** _____

❏ OCCUPATION: _____

❏ HOME: _____

❏ **NAME:** _____

❏ OCCUPATION: _____

❏ HOME: _____

GROOM'S PARENTS/STEPPARENTS

❏ **NAME:** _____

❏ OCCUPATION: _____

❏ HOME: _____

❏ **NAME:** _____

❏ OCCUPATION: _____

❏ HOME: _____

WEDDING PARTY AND RELATIONSHIP TO BRIDE OR GROOM, IF ANY

NAME	RELATIONSHIP
❏	
❏	
❏	

❏ HONEYMOON DESTINATION: _____

DESCRIPTION OF THE BRIDAL FINERY

THE GOWN: _____

_____

THE HEADDRESS/VEIL: _____

_____

THE BOUQUET: _____

_____

ATTENDANTS' DETAILS

- Check with bride's attendants to make sure any last-minute fittings or accessory purchases have been made. Make sure ushers' outfits are ready to be picked up, if rented. Make arrangements for places to dress, if necessary. Confirm arrangements for transporting wedding party to and from locations.
- Make a list of any tasks you can delegate to attendants. They may include:
  - Addressing, stamping, and mailing wedding announcements.
  - Making sure flowers are distributed after the reception.
  - Looking after children in the wedding party (flower girl, ring bearer).
- Confirm with florist delivery schedule and delivery locations for bouquets, boutonnieres, and any flowered headdresses.
- Mail or e-mail a detailed itinerary of scheduled events to your attendants. If they are arriving from out of town, confirm their accommodations. Include in the itinerary any parties they should expect to attend, as well as the recommended dress for each occasion. An itinerary might include the following.

ATTENDANTS' CHECKLIST AND ITINERARIES

BRIDE'S TELEPHONE #: _____

GROOM'S TELEPHONE #: _____

ACCOMMODATIONS: _____

ADDRESS: _____

PHONE #: _____

PICK-UP CONTACT, PRIOR TO CEREMONY: _____

TRANSPORTATION TO AND FROM CEREMONY: _____

	DATE/TIME	PLACE	DRESS	R.S.V.P.
REHEARSAL				
REHEARSAL DINNER				
BRIDESMAIDS' LUNCHEON, IF ANY				
USHERS' PRE-WEDDING GET-TOGETHER, IF ANY				
DRESSING LOCATION				
CEREMONY ARRIVAL				
WEDDING PORTRAITS				
RECEPTION				
BRUNCH				

BRIDE'S AND GROOM'S DETAILS

- Pick up wedding rings and check for fit and inscriptions. Put them away for safekeeping.
- Complete all name-change notifications and address/phone number changes (bride). Don't forget to get your marriage license.
- Confirm hair and makeup appointments, if necessary. Be sure to do a practice run with the hairdresser and makeup artist to make sure you get the look you want; decide upon the timing for hair, makeup, and dressing (bride).
- Make sure to confirm with the florist the delivery details of any bouquets or corsages for special guests and relatives.
- Finalize and wrap your gift purchases (gifts to attendants, to parents, to children, to each other).
- Continue writing thank-you notes daily, so you won't have an overload waiting for completion when you return from the honeymoon.
- Practice a few dance steps together in preparation for your reception dance.

CEREMONY AND RECEPTION DETAILS

- Make a final guest list count to give to the caterer or reception site manager. Finalize seating plans.
- Fine-tune timing for cocktails, toasts, dancing, food, beverages, and cutting the cake with caterer or reception site manager.
- Give your completed music request list to the band or DJ.
- If children are invited, plan a few activities just for them.

HONEYMOON DETAILS

- Reconfirm reservations. Make advance restaurant reservations.
- Have your honeymoon wardrobe purchased and packing list completed.
- Make sure you have procured any legal documents you may need (passport, visa).
- Make an appointment for any immunizations you and your groom need for travel in another country.
- Buy traveler's checks or make foreign money exchanges, if necessary.
- Make arrangements for ground transportation, if necessary.

KEEPING YOUR COOL

During these last few weeks before the wedding, activities may build to a fever pitch, making you feel anxious and unable to look forward to the big day in a positive way. Remain calm by taking time out each day for yourself, whether lying down for a soothing afternoon nap, exercising regularly, or practicing some form of daily meditation. Have a massage (weekly, if possible). Take time to read or go to a light-hearted movie. Listen to your favorite music. Talk regularly to the people you love (your support system), and spend quality time with your future life partner. Don't take things too seriously; laugh as much as you can. You will have avoided much stress if you have successfully been able to delegate many of the last-minute duties to vendors, friends, and family who have offered to help out.

The Final Few Weeks

CHAPTER 19

THE WEDDING DAY

B y the time the big day approaches, your wedding plans should have developed a life of their own, on track and with wheels in motion. Still, in the days before your wedding, there are a few last-minute items to attend to. Many of these details, however, can be delegated to attendants, friends, or family members ahead of time.

WEDDING DAY COUNTDOWN: PLANNING AT A GLANCE

❏ Call your reception site manager and all vendors—caterer, florist, photographers, videographers, baker, and musicians—to reconfirm arrangements and timing. ONE WEEK AHEAD

❏ Ask someone to handle any last-minute questions that your out-of-town guests might have regarding accommodations, transportation, and events.

   PERSON DELEGATED: _____

❏ Make sure that the head usher or ushers have the list of people to whom special seating or flowers will be given at the ceremony.
   ONE DAY TO ONE WEEK IN ADVANCE

❏ If you plan to give the attendants their gifts at the rehearsal or rehearsal dinner, have them wrapped and packed to go.
   ONE DAY TO ONE WEEK IN ADVANCE

❏ If you plan to give ceremony guests wedding programs, finalize them with the printer. Arrange for someone to pick up the programs from the printer. Make sure they've been given to the head usher to distribute at the wedding.
   TWO DAYS TO ONE WEEK IN ADVANCE

   PERSON DELEGATED: _____

   (CONTINUED)

❏ Assign the throwing of petals or the bubble blowing to an attendant to organize, if applicable.

ONE DAY TO ONE WEEK IN ADVANCE

PERSON DELEGATED: _____

❏ Make arrangements for clergy to be paid.

ONE DAY TO ONE WEEK IN ADVANCE

PERSON DELEGATED: _____

❏ Confirm transportation details for the wedding party.

ONE DAY TO ONE WEEK IN ADVANCE

PERSON DELEGATED: _____

❏ Confirm that the best man and honor attendant have the rings in their possession. Make sure the best man brings the marriage license to the ceremony.

ONE DAY IN ADVANCE

PERSON DELEGATED: _____

❏ If you are having a guest book, ask an attendant or relative to get it to the reception (or ceremony) site and to oversee the signing process.

PERSON DELEGATED: _____

❏ Delegate to an attendant or relative the job of taking care of the wedding gown once you leave (hanging it up, airing it out).
Don't forget to bring the gown's hanging bag to the reception site if you plan to change there— or delegate someone else to do so.

ONE DAY IN ADVANCE

PERSON DELEGATED: _____

❏ Delegate one person to be responsible for transporting to your home any gifts brought to the reception.

PERSON DELEGATED: _____

❏ Confirm any arrangements for the disposal of flowers, especially if they are being given as gifts to sick or infirm friends.

ONE DAY IN ADVANCE

(CONTINUED)

- ❏ If you plan to leave straight from the reception to your honeymoon destination, you will need to be completely packed before the wedding starts. Organize going-away clothes or assign a relative or attendant to get them ready for you.

  PERSON DELEGATED: _____

- ❏ Before you leave for the honeymoon (or before you leave from the ceremony, if you plan to travel straight from the reception to your honeymoon destination), do a spot-check for airline tickets, passports, traveler's checks, I.D.'s, calling cards, and credit cards. Be sure to pack a list of emergency phone numbers to take with you, especially if you need to check up on children or pets. Put all items in one safe place, ready to be packed in your carry-on bag.

  ONE DAY IN ADVANCE

- ❏ If you are leaving children or pets in someone's care while you're gone, call to confirm arrangements and pick-up and return dates. Give any caretakers your itinerary as well as any phone numbers. If you're leaving kids in someone's care, you will need to have them packed and ready to go before the wedding.

  If your pet will be staying away from home, make sure its food and any medications are packed to go with it.

  ONE DAY IN ADVANCE

  PERSON DELEGATED: _____

THE GLOWING BRIDE

To ensure that you will look and feel your best on the day of your wedding, make sure to get plenty of sleep the night before. Eat lightly the night before, and at breakfast and lunch if your wedding is held in the late afternoon or evening. Wedding-day jitters can wreak havoc on the digestive system, particularly one inundated with heavy, rich foods. Indulge yourself the day or morning before your wedding with a massage or facial.

- You won't have to panic when your outdoor wedding is forced indoors by inclement weather, so long as your back-up plan is in place. Go over your contingency plans in detail. Discuss where the altar, tables, and food and musicians' areas should go; make arrangements for the placement of flowers and decorations. Make sure to go over the plan detail by detail with each vendor. If it looks like your outdoor ceremony will be rained out, have a "contingency team" ready to call each vendor with the news that the wedding venue has been changed. You may even want to hold a quick rehearsal at your indoor location during the wedding rehearsal.

- If your outdoor wedding was to be held at the height of the flower-blooming season and the festivities are rained out, consider contingency plans for back-up decorations. If the garden is in your own backyard, you could have a group of friends or florists make some last-minute free-flowing arrangements. Or have a friend call a local florist or nursery the day or night before to see what's in stock, or delegate someone to visit the florist section at your local grocery store or home center to pick up some pretty hanging plants.

- Always have a back-up officiant on call in case your chosen officiant is unable to perform his duties.

- Have a back-up place to spend the wedding night lined up in case your honeymoon plans are delayed. Reserve a room in the hotel or inn where most of your guests are staying and you may not have to pay a cancellation fee.

PRE-CEREMONY PICTURES?

More and more couples today choose to see each other before the ceremony—and have their portraits taken. This means fewer portraits must be taken between the ceremony and the reception. Don't let a photographer talk you into seeing each other before the ceremony if it doesn't feel right. But do note the possible appeal of seeing each other for the first time in a more intimate setting; you'll have a chance to share some quiet moments together before the festivities begin and shorten the time set aside after the ceremony for the wedding portraits.

BRIDAL FRESHEN-UP KIT

Make a wedding-day Freshen-Up Kit to have ready to take with you to the ceremony and reception. Inside the kit, place any items you may need throughout the proceedings, such as makeup and a hairbrush to freshen up your look, and items to cover potential emergencies. Delegate an attendant or family member to be responsible for the kit. Some items you may want to consider for your kit include:

- Toothbrush, toothpaste
- Safety pins
- Extra pair of panty hose
- Makeup (lipstick, powder)
- Hair spray, hairbrush
- Tissues
- Deodorant
- Aspirin
- Small sewing kit
- Small mirror

CHAPTER 20

AFTER THE BIG DAY

RETURNING RENTALS

Designate the best man, parents, or someone reliable to see to the
return of the tuxedos and any other rentals that have been used.

STORING WEDDING ATTIRE

- **WEDDING GOWN**. Have an attendant or relative hang your
  gown up as soon as you take it off and take it to a professional
  cleaner who specializes in wedding gowns as soon as possible,
  particularly in the event of spots or champagne spills.
  The cleaners will then clean and store the gown in a sealed box or container.
  Store the box or container on a high shelf in a closet or in the attic.

- **HEADDRESS**. Any headdress not attached to a veil should
  be cleaned professionally and placed in a hatbox.

- **TRAINS AND VEILS**. Have each
  cleaned professionally with the wedding gown
  and stored in the same manner.

- **GLOVES**. For cotton gloves, launder them and then wrap in tissue in a box
  and keep in a drawer. For kid or leather gloves, have them cleaned professionally.

- **SHOES**. Carry to a shoe shop to have professionally cleaned and stored in a
  box. For cloth shoes, sponge with a cloth and mild detergent; when dry, put
  them away in tissue in a box. For leather shoes, polish and store. If tough grass
  stains are on shoes, have them cleaned professionally, no matter what the fabric.

- **BOUQUET**. If your freezer is large enough, store your bouquet inside until
  you return from your honeymoon. When you return, have it freeze-dried
  by a florist or dry it yourself by hanging it upside down in a dry place.

- **CAKE**. Make sure the caterer or baker saves the top tier
  of the wedding cake, to be stored in a box in the freezer and shared
  by the newlyweds on their first anniversary.

SELECTING WEDDING PICTURES

One of the things you should set up with your photographer and videographer before the wedding day is a date to view and select wedding photos and videos. Both you and your mate should be present to select photographs; often other family members are included.

Once you've made your selections, you will want to decide the number of each photograph printed, their order in photo albums, and how many albums you will want to order to present to family later.

CHECKLIST: PHOTO GIFT LIST

- ❏ Bride and groom
- ❏ Bride's parents
- ❏ Groom's parents
- ❏ Bride's grandparents
- ❏ Groom's grandparents
- ❏ Other relatives
- ❏ Bridal party
- ❏ Best man
- ❏ Maid/Matron of honor
- ❏ Bridesmaids
- ❏ Ushers
- ❏ Flower girl
- ❏ Ring bearer
- ❏ Special friends

Make sure the wedding negatives are stored in a safe place. You may want to have the prints scanned onto a disk or printed on a CD-ROM.

THANK-YOU NOTES

Ideally, you have kept up with your thank-you notes throughout the pre-wedding period. You will most likely be inundated with more gifts, however, on your return from your honeymoon—and thus have a whole new batch of thank-you notes to pen. Remember: Grooms write thank-you notes these days, too, so make the effort a shared task. It's a nice touch to send your parents a thank-you note and a gift, perhaps a souvenir picked out on your honeymoon excursion. Don't forget to thank your attendants for being in your wedding when you're thanking them for their gifts.

WEDDING PARTY GET-TOGETHER

A post-wedding party, hosted by the newlyweds, is a great excuse for reuniting with loved ones and close friends to remember and celebrate a shared momentous event. Whether held a month or six months after the wedding, a gathering of this kind is also a good time to view wedding videos and photo albums. It can be the most casual of affairs but can also be a chance to show off your new home, wedding gifts, and entertaining skills as a couple.

WEDDING ANNOUNCEMENTS

Although announcements are not obligatory, they serve a useful purpose. They are sent to family and friends who could not be invited to the wedding. They may also be sent to acquaintances who might wish to know of the marriage. Announcements are mailed as soon as possible, preferably the next day. Ask a friend or relative to mail them for you. Traditionally, announcements have been sent in the name of the bride's parents. It is equally appropriate today to send announcements in the names of both the bride's and groom's parents. Following is a sample of the traditional wording of a wedding announcement sent in the name of the bride's parents.

Mr. and Mrs. Harry Blair
have the honour of
announcing the marriage of their daughter
Elizabeth Sue
to
Mr. Scott Corwin Wadhams
Saturday, the fourteenth of June
one thousand nine hundred and ninety-nine
Mansfield, Pennsylvania

ADDRESS BOOK

Use this address book to keep a master list of all professional contacts and members of your wedding party.

ACCOMMODATION, ATTENDANTS': _____

    ADDRESS _____

    _____

    PHONE _____

ACCOMMODATION, HONEYMOON (#1) _____

    ADDRESS _____

    _____

    PHONE _____

ACCOMMODATION, HONEYMOON (#2) _____

    ADDRESS _____

    _____

    PHONE _____

BAKER _____

    CONTACT PERSON _____

    ADDRESS _____

    _____

    PHONE _____

    FAX _____

    E-MAIL _____

    OFFICE HOURS _____

    EMPLOYEES_____

    _____

BEST MAN _____

    ADDRESS _____

    _____

    PHONE (HOME)_____

    PHONE (WORK)_____

    FAX _____

    E-MAIL _____

BRIDAL SALON _____

    CONTACT _____

    SEAMSTRESS _____

    ADDRESS _____

    _____

    PHONE _____

BRIDESMAID #1 _____

    ADDRESS _____

    _____

    PHONE (HOME)_____

    PHONE (WORK)_____

    FAX _____

    E-MAIL _____

BRIDESMAID #2 _____

    ADDRESS _____

    _____

    PHONE (HOME)_____

    PHONE (WORK)_____

    FAX _____

    E-MAIL _____

BRIDESMAID #3 _____

ADDRESS _____

_____

PHONE (HOME)_____

PHONE (WORK)_____

FAX _____

E-MAIL _____

BRIDESMAID #4 _____

ADDRESS _____

_____

PHONE (HOME)_____

PHONE (WORK)_____

FAX _____

E-MAIL _____

BRIDESMAID #5 _____

ADDRESS _____

_____

PHONE (HOME)_____

PHONE (WORK)_____

FAX _____

E-MAIL _____

CAR/LIMOUSINE SERVICE _____

CONTACT PERSON _____

ADDRESS _____

_____

PHONE _____

FAX _____

CAR RENTAL (HONEYMOON) _____

    ADDRESS _____

    _____

    PHONE _____

    DATE _____

    CONFIRMATION NUMBER _____

CATERER _____

    CONTACT PERSON _____

    ADDRESS _____

    _____

    PHONE _____

    FAX _____

    E-MAIL _____

    OFFICE HOURS _____

    EMPLOYEES _____

    _____

CEREMONY LOCATION _____

    OFFICIAL SITE NAME _____

    CONTACT PERSON _____

    ADDRESS _____

    _____

    PHONE _____

    FAX _____

    E-MAIL _____

    OFFICE HOURS _____

    EMPLOYEES _____

    _____

FLORIST _____

   CONTACT PERSON _____

   ADDRESS _____

   _____

   PHONE _____

   FAX _____

   E-MAIL _____

   OFFICE HOURS _____

   EMPLOYEES _____

   _____

FLOWER GIRL _____

   PARENTS' NAMES _____

   ADDRESS _____

   _____

   PHONE (WORK) _____

   PHONE (HOME) _____

   FAX _____

   E-MAIL _____

HEAD USHER _____

   ADDRESS _____

   _____

   PHONE (WORK) _____

   PHONE (HOME) _____

   FAX _____

   E-MAIL _____

JEWELER (BRIDE) _____

   CONTACT PERSON _____

   ADDRESS _____

   _____

   PHONE _____

JEWELER (GROOM) _____

    CONTACT PERSON _____

    ADDRESS _____

    _____

    PHONE _____

MAID/MATRON OF HONOR _____

    ADDRESS _____

    _____

    PHONE (HOME) _____

    PHONE (WORK) _____

    FAX/E-MAIL _____

MUSICIANS (CEREMONY) _____

    ADDRESS _____

    _____

    PHONE _____

    FAX _____

    E-MAIL _____

    BUSINESS HOURS _____

MUSICIANS (OTHER) _____

    ADDRESS _____

    _____

    PHONE _____

    FAX _____

    E-MAIL _____

    BUSINESS HOURS _____

MUSICIANS (RECEPTION) _____

    ADDRESS _____

    _____

    PHONE _____

    FAX _____

    E-MAIL _____

    BUSINESS HOURS _____

OFFICIANT _____

    ADDRESS _____

    _____

    PHONE _____

    FAX _____

    E-MAIL _____

    BUSINESS HOURS _____

PHOTOGRAPHER _____

    ADDRESS _____

    _____

    PHONE _____

    FAX _____

    E-MAIL _____

    BUSINESS HOURS _____

    EMPLOYEES _____

    _____

PRINTER OR STATIONER _____

    CONTACT PERSON

    _____

    ADDRESS _____

    _____

    PHONE _____

    FAX _____

    E-MAIL _____

    BUSINESS HOURS _____

RECEPTION LOCATION _____

    SITE MANAGER _____

    ADDRESS _____

    _____

    PHONE _____

    FAX _____

REHEARSAL DINNER _____

    ADDRESS _____

    _____

    PHONE _____

    FAX/E-MAIL _____

RING BEARER _____

    PARENTS' NAMES _____

    ADDRESS _____

    _____

    PHONE (WORK) _____

    PHONE (HOME) _____

    FAX _____

    E-MAIL _____

STORE REGISTRY #1 _____

    CONTACT _____

    ADDRESS _____

    _____

    PHONE _____

STORE REGISTRY #2 _____

    CONTACT _____

    ADDRESS _____

    _____

    PHONE _____

USHER #1 _____

    ADDRESS _____

    _____

    PHONE (HOME) _____

    PHONE (WORK) _____

    FAX/E-MAIL _____

USHER #2 _____

    ADDRESS _____

    _____

    PHONE (HOME)_____

    PHONE (WORK)

    FAX/E-MAIL _____

USHER #3 _____

    ADDRESS _____

    _____

    PHONE (HOME)_____

    PHONE (WORK)_____

    FAX/E-MAIL _____

USHER #4 _____

    ADDRESS _____

    _____

    PHONE (HOME)_____

    PHONE (WORK)_____

    FAX/E-MAIL _____

USHER #5 _____

    ADDRESS _____

    _____

    PHONE (HOME)_____

    PHONE (WORK)_____

    FAX/E-MAIL _____

VIDEOGRAPHER _____

    ADDRESS _____

    _____

    PHONE _____

    FAX/E-MAIL _____

    OFFICE HOURS _____

    EMPLOYEES _____

WEDDING CONSULTANT _____

    ADDRESS _____

    _____

    PHONE _____

    FAX _____

    E-MAIL _____

    OFFICE HOURS _____

    ASSOCIATES _____

    _____

WEDDING SHOWER #1 _____

    HOST _____

    ADDRESS _____

    _____

    PHONE _____

WEDDING SHOWER #2 _____

    HOST _____

    ADDRESS _____

    _____

    PHONE _____

OTHER PROFESSIONAL SERVICES _____

    NAME _____

    ADDRESS _____

    _____

    PHONE _____

    FAX _____

    E-MAIL _____

QUICK PLANNER

This time line is a basic guide for the bride and groom. The timing and components may vary, depending upon the length of the engagement, the locale, and the type and size of the wedding.

THE FIRST STEPS:
12–24 MONTHS BEFORE

- ❏ Tell your families and friends about your engagement.
  Announce engagement in newspaper, if desired.
- ❏ Decide on the type (formality) of your wedding.
- ❏ Determine your budget.
- ❏ Decide on approximate size of your guest list.
- ❏ Decide on your ceremony and reception sites; reserve both.
- ❏ Set the date and time of your wedding.
- ❏ Meet with your clergy member or officiant.
- ❏ Organize your plan: Consult with each other and your families.
  Consider working with a wedding consultant.
- ❏ Select your attendants.
- ❏ Interview and book the services of wedding professionals,
  such as caterer, florist, photographer, and musicians.

9–12 MONTHS BEFORE

- ❑ Select your wedding gown and accessories.
  Look for dresses for your bridesmaids.
- ❑ Complete the selection process of wedding professionals,
  such as cake maker, videographer, and limousine services.
- ❑ Make arrangements for your ceremony and reception.
- ❑ Complete the guest list (full names and addresses).
- ❑ Make reservations for your honeymoon, as necessary, in advance.
- ❑ Make arrangements for you rehearsal and rehearsal dinner.
- ❑ Enroll with bridal gift registries at specialty and/or department stores.
- ❑ Record gifts as received and write thank-you notes promptly.

6–9 MONTHS BEFORE

- ❑ Finalize guest list, if not already done.
- ❑ Order your invitations, announcements, personal stationery,
  and any printed accessories and invitation enclosures.
  Obtain envelopes from printer in advance.
- ❑ Select/order bridesmaids' dresses and accessories.
- ❑ Select groom's and ushers' wedding attire; schedule rentals,
  as necessary.
- ❑ Assist mothers with selection of their outfits.
- ❑ Make arrangements for your rehearsal and rehearsal dinner.
  Notify attendees of schedule.
- ❑ Plan/reserve accommodations and activities for out-of-town
  guests and attendants, as necessary.

2–6 MONTHS BEFORE

- ❑ Address wedding invitations and announcements; buy/affix
  postage stamps.
- ❑ Make remaining decisions about ceremony and reception.
- ❑ Choose gifts for attendants and for each other.
- ❑ Select/order wedding rings; have rings engraved.
- ❑ Set dates for blood test and marriage license.
- ❑ Make any beauty appointments for the wedding day.
- ❑ Plan any parties for attendants.

1-2 MONTHS AHEAD

- ❏ Have final fitting of your gown and accessories.
- ❏ Have your portrait taken, if desired.
- ❏ Assemble and mail wedding invitations.
- ❏ Mail your wedding announcement to any newspapers, in keeping with publishing deadlines.
- ❏ Apply for/obtain your marriage license, when required by your locale.
- ❏ Reconfirm honeymoon plans; pay final deposits.
- ❏ Do any shopping for "going away" outfit and honeymoon.
- ❏ Make plans for necessary financial, address, or name changes.
- ❏ Make sure attendants have their outfits in order: purchased, altered, rented.
- ❏ If a flower girl and ring bearer are participating, confirm that their outfits are in order.

THE FINAL WEEKS

- ❏ Reconfirm rehearsal plans with clergy member and dinner site coordinator. Remind all attendees of time and place.
- ❏ Finalize seating plans for the reception.
- ❏ Have final consultations with caterer (head count) and other professionals, as necessary.
- ❏ Have any parties with attendants (bridesmaids' luncheon, bachelor or bachelorette party).
- ❏ Review best man's duties with him.
- ❏ Prepare list of any special ceremony seating for guests to give to ushers.
- ❏ Prepare list of "must have" photos and videos for the photographer and videographer.
- ❏ Pack for honeymoon.
- ❏ Make final arrangements for you and attendants for the day of the wedding: where and when to dress and assemble; get details in order for transportation to ceremony and receptions.
- ❏ Give addressed wedding announcements to whomever will be mailing them shortly after the wedding.

Quick Planner

CALENDAR

MONTH: _____

MONTH: _____

MONTH: _____

MONTH: _____

Calendar

259

NAME _____

ADDRESS _____

PHONE _____

RELATIONSHIP _____

WEDDING GIFT _____

SHOWER GIFT _____

ATTENDING (Y/N)	NUMBER OF PEOPLE	SEND MAP
RSVP DATE	**SHOWER THANK YOU**	**WEDDING THANK YOU**

NAME _____

ADDRESS _____

PHONE _____

RELATIONSHIP _____

WEDDING GIFT _____

SHOWER GIFT _____

ATTENDING (Y/N)	NUMBER OF PEOPLE	SEND MAP
RSVP DATE	**SHOWER THANK YOU**	**WEDDING THANK YOU**